In-Depth Police Dispatching

~Second Edition~

L. Tamsray

D1707656

Table of Contents

Foreword

Foreword

A dispatcher is a civil servant employee who communicates with the public, with police officers, with fire departments, with paramedics, and with numerous other contacts. Many titles are given to dispatchers: public safety dispatcher, police dispatcher, university dispatcher, fire dispatcher, call taker, 911 operator and more. This book zeroes in on police dispatching – a person whose job entails regularly communicating with police officers. While police dispatchers do sometimes communicate with paramedics, firefighters or ambulance personnel as well as utility companies, hospitals, and towing companies, their main job is communicating with police officers, and that is this book's focus.

A police dispatcher takes 911 calls as well as general and non-emergency phone calls. The police dispatcher generates complaints in the computer (or 'CAD' which stands for Computer Aided Dispatch), sends police officers to those calls and keeps track of the officers while they're on scene. Then they finally close out the calls with a disposition once those calls are resolved and all of the officers have cleared. There is a lot that goes into this job, and this book will help you to gain a real understanding of what police dispatching is really like.

Dispatching is not for everyone. I have trained employees who have seen the multi-tasking that is required and they decide that it is just too much for them to handle. At any given moment you can be answering 911, running a person's name to check for a warrant for one Officer out on the road and writing down another Officer's location as he's calling it in over the radio – and more, all at once. Dispatching can be very fast-paced and it requires a great deal of focus especially under pressure. Most callers are calling you on what is essentially the worst day of their lives because of a traumatic incident (car accident, assault, house fire etc.) and therefore dispatchers talk to a lot of hysterical, stressed-out people on the phone. The ability of a dispatcher to remain calm is essential, particularly when callers are often far from calm. Being exposed to that level of hysteria constantly isn't for everyone, especially when you factor in the fast-paced aspect of the job. I once trained a person for six months and then on her first day flying solo she couldn't handle the pace and she quit on the spot. It happens. Another trainee resigned during the training time period because she had answered a phone call about a child being sexually abused. All it took was that one phone call to convince her that dispatching was not for her. Being exposed to heartbreaking phone calls isn't easy. Another trainee just could not 'get' dispatching down. She had trouble mastering routine questions to ask callers. It really is a lot for anyone to learn and for this particular trainee, it was just too much. On the flip side, I've also had trainees who were not sure that dispatching was for them, only to have them fall in love with the job because they like helping people. It feels nice to help people, even if you're not out there in the field or out on the road helping them. Being that calm and reassuring voice on the phone for a hysterical caller and then hearing a 'thank you, thank you so much' is enough to make anyone's day.

If you're thinking of getting into dispatching as a career, this book will provide a wealth of tips on how to do the job well. If you're a newly hired dispatcher and want to learn the ins and outs of the job then this book will give you a real leg up on the learning process. Dispatching can be an incredibly rewarding career, and this book will help you to not only succeed at dispatching but to excel at it as well.

Part 1 – Call Taking

Chapter One – What's the Nature of the Call?

People call 911 for many reasons. It could be an actual emergency such as a robbery in progress or it could be just a simple question that is nowhere near an emergency. Oh, it happens alright! I work in New York State in an area that gets pummeled with snow every winter, and some municipalities have a winter parking ban which forbids any vehicles from parking on the roadway in the middle of the night so that our roads can be plowed and salted/sanded. The municipality I work for is one of those areas. It is physically impossible for a person to enter our jurisdiction without seeing a sign about the winter parking ban, which starts on November 1st. Every time Halloween rolls around, people call 911 and say: "This isn't an emergency, but can I park in the street tonight?" Lots of people. Every single year. But if it, in fact, is a serious call then as a dispatcher you have a lot of information to obtain from the caller.

Let's say you get a call about a robbery that just occurred at one of the local convenience stores, we'll use 7-11 because they're a well-known national convenience chain. It might sound something like this:

911: "911, what is the address of your emergency?"

Caller: "I'm at the 7-11 on Main Street, I was just robbed!"

911: "Is the person who robbed you still in the store?"

Caller: "No, he took the candy bar and left."

911: "Did he have a weapon?"

Caller: "No not at all. He just grabbed the candy bar off of the shelf and walked out without paying!"

Wait a minute, that's not a robbery! What the clerk is reporting is actually a larceny, specifically shoplifting. A robbery is either committed with a weapon (or the implication or threat of having a weapon) or it is committed by 'strong arm' which means physical force. No robbery occurred, but since we still have a crime that occurred we'll need more information for our officers who will be responding to the call.

911: "What was the male wearing?"

Caller: "A black jacket and some blue jeans."

911: "Did he get into a car or did he walk or bike away from the store?"

Caller: "He got into his car alone. A blue Ford Fusion."

911: "Do you have a license plate on the vehicle?"

Caller: "No."

911: "What direction did he go?"

Caller: "North."

911: "Okay, he went north on Main Street. So towards North Avenue?"

Caller: "No, towards South Street"

So the vehicle is actually heading south on Main Street. The caller does not know his directions very well but you were smart enough to verify the direction of travel by giving the closest main road name as a reference.

911: "What did the male look like?"

Caller: "He was a younger kid, maybe 19 years old. White. Kinda skinny."

911: "I'm sending an Officer now to check the area and to take a report."

911 over the police radio: "Larceny just occurred at the 7-11 on Main Street. Suspect is a white male, late teens or early 20's wearing a black jacket and blue jeans, suspect drove southbound on Main Street towards South Street in a blue Ford Fusion unknown plate."

All of that information exchanged with the caller and you end up saying just two sentences over the radio! You gathered all of the pertinent information and relayed it to your officers. Now they know to look for a blue Ford Fusion heading south on Main Street, being driven by a lone white male in his late teens or early 20's wearing a black jacket and blue jeans.

If it was, in fact, a robbery – that is if the kid took the candy bar after pointing a gun at the clerk – then that is the first thing you want to relay to your officers! Not the brand of the candy bar that was taken, not the clerk's name…the officers need to know that a weapon was involved and what kind. You are the officers' lifeline. You may be sitting at a desk in a call center but always think to yourself: "What would I want to know if I were responding to this call?" Wouldn't you approach a suspect differently if you knew that he had a gun? I know I would.

Another scenario that callers report being "robbed" is when they return home from a two-week cruise vacation and find their back door open. They've already gone inside and found that all of their electronics and jewelry have been stolen and then they called 911 to report being "robbed." What actually happened is that they were burglarized at some point in the past two weeks. Remember: a robbery is when someone takes something while using a weapon (or a perceived weapon) or by using force. A burglary is when a person illegally enters a dwelling to commit a crime, usually theft. A larceny also took place because items were taken. This is a past tense crime; there is no threat of the burglar being on scene with a crowbar that could hurt someone. That you might put out over the radio as: "Past tense burglary occurred within the past two weeks, complainant reports returning from vacation to an open door and has already checked the house and found no one inside, but items were stolen." You can also advise the caller to not touch anything in the event that fingerprints could be found.

Determining the nature of the call is important, especially when most civilians are not familiar with the titles of laws. Your job as a dispatcher is to get as much information as possible while keeping everyone's safety in mind. Sure there are calls that don't even require a police response such as inquiries of what time the Independence Day parade begins or how someone pays a parking ticket they received. But for calls that do require a police response: keep everyone's safety in mind!

Physical descriptors are important too. If I want a caller to describe a person I follow the same formula every time: sex, race, hair, face, height, body type, shirt, pants, and then shoes. By going 'top to bottom' I'm ensuring that I'm not missing anything and the caller is able to check for (or recall) one thing at a time. Some callers may not remember if a man had brown hair or blond hair but they may remember that he had a big bushy beard. Some callers even volunteer 'he had a snake tattoo' or other unique characteristics such as birthmarks or scars. In some events, I'll even ask callers what they themselves are wearing because if the caller is a female and the police are being sent somewhere to check on a suspicious female then we want to eliminate our caller as the suspicious person. With vehicles, I try to get a make, model, and license plate but if a caller isn't familiar with vehicle manufacturers then I'll ask what color the vehicle is and whether it is a car, SUV, or truck. I also ask how many doors the vehicle has. All of this information will help the officers locate the person or vehicle in question as quickly as possible.

Some callers exaggerate the severity of a situation, and I think that for the most part, it isn't intentional on their part. They aren't familiar with the 'legal lingo' (robbery vs larceny) and other callers just don't report incidents often enough to be able to accurately describe the issue that they're calling about. Sometimes a person will call me and tell me that their neighbor 'has a big fire in the yard' when in reality it ends up being a man sitting next to a fire pit with one log on it. He's having a cigar and it is actually the smell of the cigar that's bothering the caller because their home's windows are open and the smoke is drifting in. However, the way the caller initially described it, a person might imagine a garage up in flames. Then there are callers who intentionally exaggerate the severity of a situation. If a jurisdiction has a lot of serious calls such as shootings or arsons and someone calls the police about a man going through their garbage cans out at the curb then the police need to prioritize a shooting call over a garbage picker; even if the garbage picker call came in first. Callers know this, and so they sometimes call the police back and claim that the garbage picker has a knife or a gun, or that the man ate bath salts and is acting crazy. This is done in an effort to get the police to respond quicker if the caller thinks that the police are taking too long. You'll want to update your officers on any additional information that you receive from callers, even if you suspect the caller is fibbing. If the garbage picker has indeed eaten bath salts and is waving a knife or gun around then that would be a huge officer safety issue.

Another type of call where the nature of the call isn't correctly given is a kidnapping or abduction of a child. I've had children's mothers call me and say: "My son has been kidnapped," when really the child's father is three minutes late dropping the boy off at the designated location as per the custody agreement. That's quite different than a child being stolen from a department store by a stranger and thrown into a suspicious van. Making that distinction is important for your officers so they are informed ahead of time what they're going to be responding to, whether it is a potential kidnapping crime scene or a simple custody dispute.

Sometimes a caller will report that their vehicle was stolen, but it does not always turn out that the vehicle was actually stolen. Occasionally the caller lent their car to a friend and the friend hasn't returned yet or hasn't returned by the agreed-upon time. That isn't a stolen vehicle; that is the Unauthorized Use of a Vehicle or UUV. In most cases, it is a misdemeanor (unless the person who borrowed the vehicle has been convicted of UUV within the previous ten years, then it is a felony offense. It is also a felony offense if the person committed a felony crime while using the vehicle). If someone had actually stolen the vehicle that is grand larceny and that is a felony in my State. Other times the vehicle hasn't been stolen at all - a spouse may have switched parking spots or the vehicle could have been repossessed. If you run the plate through the DMV and if it was repossessed then that information would be reflected, and that quick action is going to save an officer a lot of time that he'd spend completing a stolen vehicle report unnecessarily.

Assault and harassment are confusing to callers at times, too. Harassment can carry a charge as low as a violation and, for aggravated harassment, as high as a felony charge. Assault can be a misdemeanor charge or felony charge. To put it simply: if

I pushed you that would be harassment. If you were seriously injured from that push then that would be assault. Callers who state that they've been 'assaulted' could have been pushed, shoved, punched or even kicked and unless they were seriously injured then it would still have only been harassment. Now if the caller had been hit with an object and they were seriously injured then it would be an assault. That is an important distinction because it changes the charge. Plus if the person who used that object as a weapon is still on scene then that could be an officer safety issue. You want to keep your officer's safety in mind so he isn't walking into an offender who is holding a baseball bat after just having committed an assault.

It's not only important to determine the nature of the call but to determine if the incident is in progress, just occurred, or if the incident happened in the past. The above scenario of a family's home being burglarized while they were on vacation is a good example of a past-tense crime. Of course, to be safe I'd still send two officers to that house if since the residents found an open door even though the family had already checked the house because I know that criminals will hide in crawl spaces and behind furniture and under beds. But the actual burglary had still taken place in the past, which would be very different than a child calling 911 for help because a burglar had just broken a window and was still in the family's home. In that case, it would be a crime in progress. And if the burglar had broken in, stole the tv and then left then the crime would have 'just occurred.' It is a small distinction but an important distinction for your officers because it determines their level of response.

When determining the nature of a call don't discount multiple callers who are calling about the same incident. If someone driving on the highway calls you to report passing two cars that had been involved in an accident and tells you there don't appear to be any injuries: that's fine. But when another person calls about the same accident you should never assume that the new caller is going to give you information identical to the first caller's information. You need to ask that new person if they can see if anyone is injured, because they may be closer to the victims than the last caller was and they might be able to tell if someone who was previously conscious is now unconscious, or maybe they can tell you if it looks like airbags have been deployed. Multiple callers for the same incident can seem excessive, but if you're dealing with an active shooter scenario then maybe the fifteenth caller will be the one to tell you that the shooter appears to have run out of ammunition. That's an important update for your officers.

Chapter Two – Location, Location, Location!

911 rings. It could be an elderly person who mistakenly dialed 911 instead of 411 to check the weather report, or it could be a parent of a child who shot himself while playing with a relative's unsecured firearm. The caller could be calling about anything in the world but the first thing you need to find out is location, location, location!

"911, what is the address of your emergency?" should be the first thing you say when answering 911. Don't say: "911, what is your address?" because panicked people will give you their OWN address, which is not always the same address where help is needed. If you ask: "Where are you?" callers can and do reply with: "In my house," or "I'm at work," without realizing that you do not know them, therefore, you do not know where their house or their work is located. Panicked people tend to forget that sort of thing.

Most 911 phone systems do have call mapping capabilities; the phone rings and a map comes up on the dispatcher's screen with the caller's location. However, in my area, that's only if the caller is calling from a landline.

If the caller is calling from a cell phone, then the closest cell phone tower's address shows on the map, which is not usually where the caller actually is. And all cell phone calls in my county go to one large call center (which is not in my jurisdiction) and those dispatchers then transfer the calls to the proper agency. A lot of 911 calls end up not being emergencies at all, but in a true emergency what would you rather do: talk to two different dispatchers in two different jurisdictions before help is sent, or talk to one dispatcher who sends help right away?

My #1 tip if you ever need to call 911 is to do it from a landline if possible, and my #2 tip is to program your local police department's phone number into your cell phone and to call that number instead of 911 if you're calling from a cell phone. Because you'll likely be speaking to the same person that the first call center would have transferred your 911 call to anyhow. I know because I have had 911 callers transferred to me from the large call center outside of my jurisdiction only to have callers ask me for the non-emergency number of my jurisdiction. The callers thank me from the 911 line, hang up, and then call me on the non-emergency line without ever realizing that they're speaking to the same person.

911 technology aside…it is absolutely imperative to get the physical address of the emergency.

What if a physical address isn't known? What if a small child calls you with an emergency and doesn't know the address?

Here is how a call like that might play out:

911: "911, what is the address of your emergency?"

Child: "I can't wake up Grandpa."

911: "Are you at your Grandpa's house?"

Child: "Yes. He isn't waking up though."

911: Do you know your Grandpa's address?"

Child: "No."

911: "Is there a Grandma home?"

Child: "No but Grandpa won't wake up."

911: "Okay, do you have a brother or sister with you at Grandpa's house?"

Child: "No it is just me and Grandpa."

911: "Do you know how to read?"

Child: "Yes."

911: "Okay, look for a piece of mail for me. It can be a magazine or a letter. Any mail with your Grandpa's name on it. Can you do that?"

Child: "I can't find any! Grandpa wake up! Wake up, Grandpa!"

911: "What street does Grandpa live on? Do you know?"

Child: "Main Street, I think."

911: "Can you go outside and look at the numbers on the house for me?"

Child: "Okay...it says 97."

911: (Searching for a history of 97 Main Street, finds a Joe Smith as the resident) "Is your grandpa's name Joe Smith?"

Child: "Yes."

And finally, the address is known so you can get resources started that way while also guiding the child to find out if Grandpa is breathing and how to do CPR or to find an adult neighbor to do CPR if needed. Alternatively you could have asked the child for Grandpa's name and then tried running a search, however, if Grandpa's name really was Joe Smith then you could have found many Joe Smiths and you would have no way of knowing which Joe Smith is the child's grandfather. Or maybe the child knows his home phone number and you could have had another dispatcher call the child's parents to get Grandpa's address.

It isn't always a child who doesn't know an address, though. How do you get an address on a highway from an adult if there's a motor vehicle accident? Ask callers for mile markers, what the highway is called, whether it's a highway that goes north or south or east or west, if they're between two exits and what those exits are called or numbered, or if there are any businesses or landmarks visible from the highway.

What if a pedestrian was struck in the roadway at an intersection? Then you find out what two streets intersect and what businesses are nearby; anything to determine the proper location.

Local landmarks are helpful in determining a location too. This is why the ride-alongs I've mentioned are helpful to go on because you can see all of your jurisdiction's landmarks live in person.

Just remember that landmarks can be referred to by different names by different generations. We have four school buildings in our jurisdiction. One hasn't been an actual school since before I was a kid but people in their sixties and older still call it 'Jefferson School' even though today it is a multi-use building with a café and luxury apartments. Everyone under sixty or so just refers to this place as 1 Main Street because the building is the first one on Main Street. We also have a school called Kennedy School and it is on Jefferson Street which is on the opposite side of the town from the 1 Main Street building. Once our Chief was off-duty and he called out over the radio for officers to check on a suspicious person at 'Jefferson School' so the patrols (all in their late twenties or early thirties) went to Kennedy School because it is on Jefferson Street. They've never known 1 Main Street as Jefferson School so they went to the school on Jefferson Street. Of course, these aren't the real names of our landmarks or streets but I'm sure every town has a similar lexicon of their own. Businesses close and new ones open in the same location. In just under ten years we've had one building that has housed five different restaurants under five different names. Let's use national chain names to simplify: the same building has been a KFC, a Dunkin Donuts, an Arby's, a Subway and a Wendy's, all in the course of ten years. If someone out of state calls the police here for a welfare check on a family member that they can't get a hold of and they weren't sure of the name of the family member's street but knew it was the side street next to Dunkin Donuts then the dispatcher might not know where to send help because Dunkin Donuts hasn't been in this town for eight years. Pinning down a location is necessary and sometimes it takes some detective work.

What if a caller isn't cooperative about their location? A lot of times callers are panicked and will only keep repeating: "Just send help!" without answering your questions, and that's when you need to tell the caller that you can only send help if you know where to send it. Getting the location of the emergency is the first and more important part of call taking.

Sometimes callers assume that you know where they are. I've had people call me and say: "You better send a car over to check this guy outside of thirty-one, he seems suspicious," and my next question is: "Thirty-one what?" If the call came in on my non-emergency line then all I see on the Caller ID is a phone number, occasionally a name too. On my non-emergency line, I never see an address on the Caller ID. And if that person used a cell phone to call 911 to report this suspicious man then I'd see a cell phone tower's address, which I've already explained isn't always where the caller is. Just remember that every agency is different. I work for two different agencies and at one agency we have both a 911 phone system and a traditional phone system whereas at the other agency all calls go to the same large phone which includes 'lines' for 911 as well as 'lines' for non-emergency calls. If I'm working at the other agency then I do see people's names and addresses on the screen – but not always. Sometimes I see just an intersection and while that may be close to where the caller is calling from it is not necessarily where they want the police to go.

The caller could be calling from one side of town but might need the police to go to the other side of town. An example of that is when a friend gets a text message from someone saying they're in trouble and to have the police come because that person can't call for help themselves. You would want to send officers to the friend in need, not the friend who got the text message. And in this particular situation, you'd definitely want to check the history of the friend in need and the address that you're sending the officers too because a lot of times these calls tend to be domestic disputes in progress and usually some intoxicated people too which could be dangerous for your officers.

You need to get the correct location of a call from your callers using any method possible. If you're dealing with an adult and the caller knows the street but not the numerical address then ask for what section of the block it is: is it between North and

South streets or further up near First and Second streets? If the caller doesn't know the street: ask for a landmark.

Children can provide pretty good information if you ask them for it. Kids are able to tell you what color a house is or what color their mother's car is and if it is parked in front of the house. They might even be able to read license plate numbers to you over the phone, which you could then run in the computer in order to find the mother's address. Kids do best with simple, one-at-a-time questions. "What color is your house?" is better than: "What color is your house, what color is your mom's car, what color shirt is the man wearing that's pounding on your door?" because smaller children can mix up their answers.

In our town we have two senior living centers, so we tend to get a lot of calls from seniors who have fallen and need help getting up. Some of these calls come in from monitoring services but sometimes the staff calls the police and sometimes the fallen senior calls for themselves. These buildings are over five floors, so getting an apartment number or a room number is crucial. We can't help that senior up off the floor if we can't find them, so those room numbers or apartment numbers are essential.

Every jurisdiction has rental properties and we are no exception. We have a couple of high-rise rental properties that have numerous apartments inside. We'd need an apartment number for calls in these buildings, or a floor number at the very least. We also have single-family homes that have been converted into rental properties that house both upper and lower tenants, so a dispatcher would need to ask if help was needed in the upper or the lower. The next town over has a lot of side-by-side duplexes, some share an address with a directional such as 123 Main Street, South. Other duplexes use letters to distinguish apartments such as 'A' or 'B'. If you receive any call where police are requested at any multi-resident building then you need to get a room number, apartment number, North, South, 'A', 'B', upper or lower.

Sometimes we get calls reporting a child or a dog inside of a parked car. This is usually in the summer but it can happen any time of year. In the summer especially, the temperature inside of a parked car with no A/C running can be fatal for a child or a pet. If the vehicle is parked at a grocery store then odds are it is a pretty big parking lot – so in addition to asking for the vehicle's make, model, color and license plate you'll want to find out where in the lot it is parked. Is the car parked in the main lot, or the smaller lot off to the side of the grocery store? Is it parked near a cart port? Is it parked in a fire lane, handicapped spot or near a lamp post? Is there a grocery store employee or someone else there who can wave at officers when they arrive and direct them to the car in question?

Schools have gymnasiums and auditoriums and classrooms, shopping malls have many stores inside and sometimes several levels, movie theaters have several big screens and restaurants have patios and kitchens. Use any method you're able to in order to get a good location for your officers to respond to.

Chapter Three – Hot Calls

There are the types of calls that every dispatcher hopes to never get in his career and one of those types of calls is an active shooter / active assailant. With so many lives at stake, it can be difficult to remain being that calm, cool and collected voice on the phone for an understandably hysterical caller who is experiencing the most terrifying moments in her life. And when one of these types of incidents occur your phones will be ringing non-stop, which only adds to the stress of the situation.

An active shooting is sometimes called a 'school shooting' but as recent events have shown these incidents can take place anywhere. They can happen in a movie theater, a shopping mall, a school or university or any place that there are a large number of people...anywhere that an assailant has unrestricted access to a large number of people.

Some examples of active shooters in American history:

On February 14, 2018, a shooter opened fire at Marjory Stoneman Douglas High School (Florida). He killed seventeen students and staff members and injured another seventeen people. The shooter escaped the scene and was arrested a short time later.

On November 5, 2017, there was a mass shooting at the First Baptist Church in Sutherland Springs (Texas). Twenty-six people were killed and twenty others were injured. After being shot twice by an armed citizen, the assailant fled in a vehicle and crashed after a high-speed chase. The shooter was found deceased with multiple gunshot wounds, including a self-inflicted headshot.

On October 1, 2017, there was the Las Vegas shooting (Nevada) when a gunman opened fire on a musical festival's crowd. Fifty-eight people were killed and another 851 people were injured. The shooting lasted ten minutes before the shooter committed suicide.

On June 12, 2016, there was a shooting at an Orlando nightclub (Florida). Forty-nine people were killed and another fifty-three people were injured. The incident turned into a hostage situation where the shooter was ultimately met with deadly force by the police.

On December 2, 2015, at the Inland Regional Center in San Bernadino (California) a married couple carried out a mass shooting and attempted bombing at a company Christmas party. Fourteen people were killed and another twenty-two were injured over two or three minutes. After fleeing the scene the couple was later killed during a shootout with police where officers were injured.

On December 14, 2012, there was a shooting at Sandy Hook Elementary School (Connecticut). Twenty children were shot and killed and six adult staff members were shot and killed. The assailant had killed his mother in her home before going to the school. The shooter then committed suicide after killing the students and staff at the elementary school.

On April 16, 2007, a school shooting occurred at Virginia Polytechnic Institute and State University (Virginia). Thirty-two people were killed and seventeen people were wounded. The shooter committed suicide.

On April 20, 1999, a school shooting occurred at Columbine High School (Colorado). Two students murdered twelve students and one teacher and injured twenty-one others. Police exchanged gunfire with the pair before the two of them committed suicide. In addition to shootings, the attack also involved a firebomb, propane tanks converted to bombs, ninety-nine explosive devices and car bombs.

On October 16, 1991, a mass shooting occurred at Luby's Cafeteria (Texas). The assailant drove his pick-up truck through the front window of the restaurant before he began shooting. Twenty-three people were killed and twenty-seven were injured. After a brief shootout with the police, he committed suicide by shooting himself.

On August 20, 1986, the Edmond post office (Oklahoma) had a mass shooting where an employee killed fourteen co-workers and injured another six co-workers before committing suicide, all in under fifteen minutes.

On July 18, 1984, at a McDonald's restaurant in San Diego (California) a man shot and killed twenty-one people and injured nineteen others before being fatally shot by law enforcement.

On August July 31, 1966, a man stabbed his wife and his mother to death in Texas. The following day, August 1, the man went to an observation deck of the Main Building tower at the University of Texas at Austin and opened fire on the surrounding campus and streets. In ninety minutes he shot and killed sixteen people and injured thirty-one others. A civilian and a police officer fatally shot the assailant.

There are sadly many other examples of mass shootings, too many to list here. I have not named any of the assailants because I do not believe that their names should receive any attention. I feel that part of these people's motivations to commit these horrible acts may stem from a desire to obtain notoriety and fame, and I feel that by naming them I would be giving them 'credit' for these horrific acts and that's not something I'm willing to do.

Active shootings end when either: 1) the assailant has run out of ammunition, 2) the assailant is apprehended via surrender or is stopped by the police with force (sometimes deadly force) or 3) the assailant commits suicide. Very rarely do assailants escape. Most active shootings are over within fifteen minutes.

As a dispatcher, you'll want to get as much information as possible from each caller, no matter how many 911 calls you take in the process. The first fifteen callers may alert you that shots have been fired but they may not know by whom or with what type of weapon. The sixteenth caller might be able to tell you that the shooter has run out of ammunition.

Most agencies include active shooter scenarios in dispatcher training. Just like other crimes in progress you want to determine if the scene is safe for your officers and other emergency personnel and you want to obtain a description of the suspect(s). Be sure to follow your agency's protocol for call taking when you get a call for an active shooter. The following is not an official protocol, it is a general guide of what sort of information you would want to gather in the event of an active shooter incident:

What is the address of the emergency?

Is it a school? A shopping mall? Some other type of location?

Where is the shooter? Is there more than one?

If in a building such as a school: what floor? What room or area in the school is the shooter?

What type of weapons are involved?

Long gun? Pistol? Knife? Explosives?

Did the shooter(s) leave?

Did he/they leave on foot, on a bicycle, in a car etc.?

What direction did he/they go?

What is the description of the vehicle?

What is the description of the shooter(s)?

Get a sex and race, age, clothing description, hair color etc.

Is the shooter wearing any sort of bullet-proof vest, etc?

Are there any hostages?

How many? Where are they?

Is anyone injured?

What are the types/extent of injuries?

Some locations have policies in place for active shooters, such as schools. The people at the location in question can either evacuate if it is safe to do so or they may go into 'lockdown' depending on the location's policy.

If the caller feels it is safe to leave then he should get out. If the caller can take a route that won't cross the assailant's path, then that's the best route for the caller to take. If the caller gets outside and sees the police he should keep his hands where the officers can see them.

If the location is a school (for example) and goes into 'lockdown' then odds are the students and teachers have had lockdown drills in the past. People gather in the nearest room with a locking door and barricade it with anything possible. Windows/blinds are shut and the lights are turned off so that the people will be harder to see. Everyone should be very quiet and silence their cell phones. They should not answer the door for anyone, even if the person is crying to be let it, because it can very well be the assailant on the other side of the door.

When an active shooter call happens, dispatch centers are inundated with phone calls. You will get calls from the location itself from many different people. People who live nearby may also call to report hearing shots fired or explosives detonated. Other agencies will call to see if they can help at the scene. News stations and other media will call to find out what is happening. Family and friends of the people on location will call requesting information regarding their loved ones' safety. It is your job to remain calm and to gather as much information as possible and to continuously update your officers with that information.

Other 'hot' calls include robberies. While some callers are panicked and often misreport a shoplifting/larceny or past-tense burglary incident as a 'robbery' (mentioned earlier) there are true robberies that happen at convenience stores, banks, street corners or elsewhere. Most businesses have a 'panic' or 'hold up' button that they can press to silently alert their alarm company to call the police, and as a dispatcher, I've taken several of those calls from the alarm companies. While those silent alarm buttons are invaluable for the staff at the business who may not be able to call the police themselves at that moment in time, it does not give me much information about what is happening at that business. Is there a robbery in progress? Does the person have a weapon, or did he imply that he has a weapon? The alarm company won't know, because their job is to inform the police that the alarm has been activated. Some robberies are 'strong arm' robberies where physical force is used by the offender but armed robberies are the ones where you need to determine what sort of weapon is involved so that your officers know what they're going to be dealing with. You'll also need to obtain a description of the offender including sex, race, height, clothing and any other distinguishing features such as any tattoos or a bandana tied around the face. Find out what the person took from the victim or store – if it was a case of beer and the guy ran away on foot then he'll be pretty easy to spot, but if he stuffed the contents of the cash register into a bag and hopped into a car before speeding off then he may be harder for the officers to find. You'll need to find out how the suspect left (on foot, in a car, on a bicycle, etc.) and what direction the person went. If the caller can give you license plate number that's great, but even a make/model of the vehicle or the color can be helpful for the officers who are going to try to apprehend the suspect. If the victim or anyone else has been injured you'll need to find out if they need medical care or treatment. If the suspect has touched anything in the area (cash register, door, merchandise), you can advise the caller to not touch any possible evidence. If the location of the robbery is close to your agency's border then it is always a good idea to alert your neighboring agency of the robbery's specifics such as where the robbery took place and a description of the suspect(s) as well as their getaway method of travel and last known direction. If that neighboring agency's dispatcher is monitoring other radio frequencies then they may have already heard the specifics. That dispatcher has a well-developed 'radio ear' which we'll cover in the next chapter.

Other types of 'hot' or very serious calls include hostage situations and suicidal people or a combination of those two scenarios. There is training for crisis negotiation skills for dispatchers and if it is not covered by your agency's standard training methods then you may be able to complete off-site or even online training on these topics.

Chapter Four – Proceed with Caution on These Calls

While any call has the possibility of taking a bad turn, there are certain types of calls that have a higher potential to do so: domestic disputes, welfare checks, alarm calls and open doors. Of course, there are hostage situations or active shooter situations too – but we know off the bat that those are going to be very serious calls. What about the others I've just mentioned, though? Those calls can end up 100% okay – but they also can end up with someone dying. You always have to keep that in the back of your mind with each and every call.

Domestics are a family dispute of any kind – it could be a child upset about having to follow house rules and throwing a chair at his father in protest of said rules, or it could be a husband beating his wife or anything in between. Before anything else, be sure to get the address of the occurrence. Then find out if there are any weapons on the premises or on someone's person, and ask if anyone has been drinking or using any drugs. Sometimes the police will get calls for one address two or three times a day for domestic disputes. Let's say that a male/female domestic call came in once for a simple disagreement. The wife came home late and a little tipsy and her husband is yelling at her. He had a few beers while waiting for her to get home and now he's agitated. The police arrive on the scene and he's belligerent but not dangerous. With the police's help, they both agree to keep to themselves for the night. The police leave.

A half hour later the wife, still a bit tipsy, decides to play some music in the kitchen and make a bedtime snack. She's a bit giddy, dancing around a bit. The husband is in the bedroom and can't fall asleep because of the music. He gets agitated all over again that she was out so late. He's got to get up for work and he just wants her to quiet down. He storms from the bedroom, alarm clock in hand, and into the kitchen where he throws the alarm clock at her and yells that he has to wake up for work in the morning. The alarm clock hits her on the head and cuts her forehead. She calls 911 a second time and the police return, this time with the paramedics to take care of the cut to her forehead. The wife declines to press charges and just wants her husband to go to bed and leave her alone. The husband claims the cut was an accident. Both parties again agree to stay separated for the night, so the police leave a second time.

The wife goes to bed and falls asleep while the husband decides to take a few shots of vodka to lure him to sleep. He gets into bed but can't fall asleep because his wife is now snoring. He gets madder & madder at the whole night in general and begins choking her. She wakes up, a struggle ensues and they knock over lamps which wakes up a neighbor next door. The wife struggles free and manages to run into the kitchen. The neighbor calls the police. The husband also goes into the kitchen. When the police return a third time the husband is drunk and yelling that anyone who stops him from sleeping is going to be sorry, then he grabs a knife out of the knife block and he charges at the police officers with it. He is subdued and arrested. See how the first time the call didn't seem like too big of a deal, and by the third trip to the residence, the man was charging at police with a weapon? Domestic disputes tend to escalate, whether in one night or over a period of months. A person may not have a firearm registered to them, but in the above example, one man used both an alarm clock and a kitchen knife as a weapon. And let's not forget: just because someone doesn't have a firearm permit does not mean that they didn't illegally obtain a firearm somehow.

Your job as a dispatcher is to stay on the line with the neighbor and have them give you a play-by-play of what's happening such as the couple's whereabouts in the house. Kitchens are full of knives, but someone could just as easily pick up the lid of a toilet tank in a bathroom and heave it at someone. Remember: what would you want to know before arriving on the scene? Find out as much as possible, and update the officers as you're getting the information.

Welfare checks are another type of call that can go badly in certain situations. Usually a neighbor will call the police with concern for another neighbor, such as a neighbor calling about an elderly person who normally sits on the porch in the afternoon but hasn't for three days and there are three days' worth of newspapers piled up on the porch, yet the senior's car is parked in the driveway. Police arrive on the scene and could find that the resident fell and could not reach the phone. Or perhaps the resident has passed away. Those types of welfare checks happen often, as do relatives who call from out of state because they haven't heard from a family member that lives in your jurisdiction. In those situations, you should try to find out if there is a lockbox code or a hidden key that will help the officers to get into the house to check on the person. Perhaps a neighbor has a key or a family member that lives in the area. Some police departments carry breaching kits to get into houses but some don't. Insurance may dictate whether or not police can force open a door. In some jurisdictions, the fire department can force open a door if the police ask them to, as long as the police are on the scene too. However, if a key or a lock box code can be located and used, that would be a much better option than breaking down an elderly person's door. Or there's always the possibility of an open window.

Another type of welfare check stems from social media. A person may post online that he has 'had it' and it's 'time to go.' A friend of his sees this post and she becomes concerned so she calls the police to go and check on him since he's not answering his phone or any online messages. The police arrive on the scene – sometimes the man is putting a homemade noose around his neck as the police walk in, sometimes he's calmly playing on his X-Box while his phone charges in the next room. Social media does lack 'tone' so in the X-box scenario maybe the guy was frustrated with a game and said online that he has 'had it' and when he said it was 'time to go' perhaps he meant 'it is go time' as in time to win this game. He didn't respond to the caller's messages because he wasn't near his phone. On the flip side, people absolutely attempt suicide. If the person's online profile is viewable to the public, I will check out the page myself to see the post and even look for other posts that might suggest self-harm. I'll look at his photos to see if I can find any of the man holding a firearm that he may use on the police if they try to stop him from committing suicide. I'll also check the history of his address to see if the police were called there in the past for similar incidents. For being 'just' a dispatcher, I certainly do a lot of detective work! I want to know that my officers are not walking into an unsafe scene.

I say 'just' a dispatcher because dispatchers everywhere are (at the time of this being published) frustrated about not being viewed as first responders, often our positions are considered 'clerical.' I don't know many secretaries who can guide a caller through CPR, instruct someone how to deliver a baby, or try to talk someone down who is threatening to commit suicide. If you think about it: dispatchers are the *first* first responders, because that call to 911 is the first contact a person has with law enforcement and emergency services! And just like additional firefighters, paramedics and police are called into service during a major incident such as a fire, severe weather event or civil unrest it just does not make sense to call dispatchers 'administrative' or 'clerical support' workers.

Another type of call that can go bad quickly is an alarm call. Alarm calls can be hit or miss. Sometimes you'll have a windy night and some businesses in your jurisdiction may have sensitive alarms. Nine times out of ten times those alarm activations will be a false alarm due to the wind or the rain. We actually have a discount store that has helium-filled balloons that move around due to the heating/cooling vents and that's enough to set off the interior alarms at the store. But that tenth alarm call will be a glass breakage alarm and the police may very well arrive and find that someone has smashed in the front window of a convenience store and stolen lottery tickets, cigarettes, and the cash register.

I always send two officers to alarm calls in the event that the suspect is still on scene but tries running from the police. You need one officer to stand by the now-wide-open store until an after-hours employee or emergency enclosure company can be reached to secure the store and you need one officer (preferably more) to chase the suspect. This is where you really need to keep track of your officers. An officer running with a bullet-proof vest and a utility belt full of extra weight tends to huff and puff over the radio as he's yelling out the suspect's description, clothing, and direction of travel. Listen carefully. You'll need this information in case things go south and the suspect struggles with the officer on the ground. You need to know where they are so that you can send back-up. Even if there isn't a struggle you still need this information because neighboring agencies may be monitoring your radio and may call you and ask for the information so they can join the foot pursuit. That happens a lot during serious calls or chases of any kind: you'll be monitoring suspect information, officers' locations while also answer the phone to provide that information to other agencies who call to request it. Sometimes an officer will call out a location or address that the suspect threw something (like a gun) to be retrieved by another officer while the primary officer continues the chase.

My agency has a computer program that lets me put in any address, and it gives me a wealth of information – the owner of the address, the name of the business and an after-hours contact person if it is a business, and it even tells me nearby fire hydrants. But the best feature of this program? It provides me with the backup address of any address I enter. If I enter '123 North Street' it tells me that the house directly behind it is 123 South Street. Their backyards back up to each other – helpful information if the suspect hops a fence. While one officer is chasing the suspect I can send another officer to 123 South Street who can hopefully grab the suspect as he runs down the driveway of that address. Not every agency has this program but Google maps works just as well. Think ahead, always.

Calls for open doors can be bad, too. Just like alarm calls, the wind could have blown a door open because the door wasn't latched into the frame completely. It happens. But open doors can also be on vacant houses, where a homeless drug user could be sitting inside – all hopped up on heaven knows what and ready to fight anyone he comes across. He could have needles on him too that could prick an officer's hand right through his gloves which would put that officer in danger of an infection, contact with a dangerous drug or even a disease. If my officers come across a person who is clearly someplace he shouldn't be, I always run that person's name and check his history to see if he's a drug user or if he is wanted by other jurisdictions or to find out if he tends to fight with police.

People found in vacant structures are rarely friendly, safe or sober.

I always send two officers to any call for an open door, whether it is at a business or a residence because I never know who they'll encounter. It could be a contractor working late or it could be a combative person on hallucinogens – you just never know.

Chapter Five – Other Types of Calls & Incidents

Parking complaints, barking dogs, smoke alarms, customer trouble, traffic accidents, broken down vehicles, escorts for funerals or banks, reckless drivers, shoplifting, graffiti, loud parties, stolen identities, underage drinking, bonfires, harassment, criminal mischief, confused people, drug activity, disorderly person, driving while intoxicated, using fireworks, flooded roads, water main breaks, landlord and tenant disputes, people locked out of their own homes or cars, reports of an unstable person: these are all other types of calls you may take on a daily basis.

Every agency has routine calls and a lot of those calls depend on where your jurisdiction is and what's inside of it. The main agency that I work for has no bodies of water (except for a community pool in the summertime) so we don't get calls for boating accidents or ice fishers in trouble whereas two towns north of us there is a river so that agency has a lot of calls regarding the water. We have a lot of businesses on one of our main roads and so we get a lot of fender benders since it tends to get congested during lunchtime and on weekends. Since that main road also connects us our neighboring agencies north and south of us, we get a lot of 'passing through' motorists who get tickets for speeding.

We also have three senior citizen housing buildings, so we get a lot of calls for helping up seniors who have fallen out of bed or have locked themselves out of their apartments. Sometimes the elderly call 911 to complain about the staff in the senior living buildings, or 'just to chat' and we have to tell them that is a misuse of emergency services. One senior building has assigned parking, and the seniors will call us to complain that someone has parked in their spot – even if the senior does not have a car to park in that spot.

The houses in our jurisdiction are pretty close together so we do get noise complaints year-round; in the winter people complain that their neighbor is 'shoveling too loudly' or shoveling too early in the morning and in the summer we get complaints about loud backyard parties. When you have people living so close to each other, there will be noise complaints.

Referrals are a common occurrence. Our agency also refers a lot to our local sanitation department, water department and highway department – things like stop signs that were knocked down, water main breaks that need to be repaired and even tree branches that need to be trimmed down. We also notify the State for traffic signals that are out of order or the Parks Department for concerns with playground equipment. Utility companies are contacted by us on a regular basis for street lights that are out or if a telephone pole has been damaged/downed during a motor vehicle accident. We call the gas company to shut off the gas in a house in the event of a fire or other emergency.

Often other police agencies will call me to inform me that their officers are on a traffic stop (they have pulled over a vehicle) and the driver of the vehicle has a warrant for our jurisdiction. After confirming that it is a good/valid warrant, we need to collect that person so he can go in front of a judge. The first thing I ask is if the other agency has charges against the person – because if they do then I'm not going to send one of my officers over just to wait around and then be told to disregard. If the agency does have charges they'll call us when they're all finished up; that may be in a couple of hours or if the driver committed a serious crime it could be much longer than that if he has to see a judge in that jurisdiction first. If the agency does not have charges then I will work with that agency's dispatcher to determine a halfway point for my officer to meet their officer so we can collect the warrant suspect. Or the reverse happens: we'll arrest a person for driving while intoxicated and we'll discover that the driver has a warrant for another jurisdiction. A lot of this job involves communicating with other agencies.

Our agency provides a police car escort for funeral processions to ensure that motorists are traveling safely. We also provide escorts for banks or for businesses that are carrying a lot of money to or from a bank for everyone's safety and for the security of the money.

With so many convenience stores and small retailers, we get a good number of shoplifting complaints. Sometimes we'll have a manager call and report that one of the store's employees has been stealing money out of the cash register. And when delivery trucks make their deliveries to these businesses and need help getting into the parking lot we'll temporarily stop traffic so that the truck can get in quicker and easier.

Our officers monitor traffic and students just after dismissal time at our schools. They're looking for people who are double parked or for people driving past school buses that have their flashing lights and stop signs activated. They're also monitoring student conduct to ensure that no fights are happening. Sometimes a principal or guidance counselor from a school will call the police and tell us about a possible fight occurring after school, and we'll make sure that it doesn't happen.

Overnight, not many businesses are open for business. That's when our police officers conduct premises checks, which is making sure that a business's doors are locked etc. My officers know which businesses have overnight cleaning services and which ones don't, so if a business is normally dark and locked up and my officer sees a light on and someone inside then he'll check it out to ensure that the person should be there and isn't a burglar. Just recently a barber shop installed a strobe light in their shop and it isn't on during the day. When an officer that normally works the day shift is working a night shift he'll notice the strobe light right away and call into dispatch about a possible silent alarm going off at the barber shop, and I will tell him that it is just a strobe light and that it is always on at night. Those little tidbits of information are helpful to know as a dispatcher. In this case, it would have saved the police from waking up the barber in the middle of the night to make sure that his shop is on the up-and-up. Our officers also check schools to be sure no one is loitering and they drive through our parks too to check that no one is in the parks after they've closed for the night.

We also do house checks, which is when someone is on vacation or is deployed by the armed forces. The police on every shift will drive by the resident's house to be sure that no one is there who should not be there. We do house checks for extended hospital stays too, and also for 'snow birds' who are residents who live in our jurisdiction in the spring and summer and then live someplace warmer in the fall and winter. We'll even check for burglars at the home of a family during a funeral service since most funerals are announced in the community newspaper which would let anyone reading it know when a family won't be at home. We regularly check any vacant houses in our jurisdiction to make sure that no one is trespassing inside of them.

On weekends and holidays, the police tend to get more calls for drunk drivers than they receive during the work week. Weekends and holidays also tend to bring on more noise complaints, fights, and domestic issues because of alcohol consumption.

While most agencies have routine calls it is good to keep in mind that anything can happen at any time. Sure, you're more likely to get a call for a drunk driver on a Friday night right after the bars are closing than you are if you're working during the day but there have been days I've worked when it was ten in the morning and someone was arrested for drunk driving. One time, a high-speed chase happened on a Sunday afternoon that took our police officers through several other jurisdictions.

Another time, I was working a very quiet midnight shift when a stolen truck was driven right into someone's living room at eighty miles per hour.

One dispatcher I used to work with worked the day shift only. She confided in me that she would never work an overnight shift because she was afraid something would happen that she didn't know how to handle and she'd end up looking stupid. In a way I suppose she was right; she was accustomed to getting fender bender calls and parking complaints during the day. If she had worked the overnight when the truck drove into a house and if she had to call an emergency enclosure crew to seal up the damaged house then she would not have known who to call or what their after-hours number was. That would have delayed things on the police's end because they'd be standing around waiting for her to figure out who to call and how to reach them.

This is why when you're training to be a dispatcher, you should have to work each shift a handful of times in order to get a feel for each shift's routine calls. Every dispatcher should be able to work every shift; no one should be 'afraid' of working an unfamiliar shift because anything can happen at any time. You never know when a vehicle will drive into a building when a robbery will occur, when a high-speed chase will happen or when a major weather event will occur. A good dispatcher is familiar with every type of call and situation imaginable and is prepared to take those calls and take care of those situations.

Part 2 - Dispatching

Chapter Six – Don't Assume Anything!

There are certain types of calls that might seem routine at first, but they have the potential to be much more serious. On my first day working solo after training, I got my very first 911 call ever and it went something like this:

911: "911, what is the address of your emergency?"

Child: (about 17 years old and super calm) "It is 123 Main Street. My mom needs an ambulance."

911: "What happened to your mom?"

Child: "She was using her scissors and she cut herself."

So I put the call out as 'first aid' or 'EMS' call (emergency medical service). After all, my own mother uses scissors all the time when she sews, quilts or works on other crafts. It must have been an accidental slip of the scissors, maybe she was cutting some fabric and snipped her fingertip a bit. My mistake here was that I heard the calm voice of the kid and I assumed that the scene was safe. I didn't get further information such as where on the body the mother cut herself, what she had been doing that caused the injury, whether she was conscious or not, and if the bleeding was controlled. The kid was so calm that I assumed that it was an accident, a routine first aid call. I was so wrong.

My officers arrived on scene to find a hysterical woman wielding very sharp scissors who had somewhat slit her wrists with them in an attempt to commit suicide. There was a lot of blood in the living room. Officers got blood on them while trying to get the scissors away from the mentally distraught woman. Quite different than the minor sewing accident I had imagined! After everyone was safe and the woman was on her way to the hospital in an ambulance, the Lieutenant in charge came back to the call center and told me what had actually happened. Well, she didn't "tell" me, she actually screamed at me, and rightfully so! I neglected to get the specifics and by doing that I had put lives at risk. The life of the kid who called me, the life of the mother who might have panicked when the police arrived and could have tried to slit her throat, and the lives of the officers who could have easily been stabbed with the scissors. Of course, the officers are trained to deal with mentally distraught people or with people who have a weapon, but that information is very helpful to know up front before they respond to the call. If the paramedics had arrived on the scene before the police: would they have the training necessary to deal with a distraught and unstable person with a weapon? Never assume anything with any call; ask questions and get the facts. Get as much information as you can for the safety of everyone.

Not long after that first 911 call and my well-deserved reprimand, I got another 911 call which sounded basic too. The agency I work for does not dispatch the fire department or the paramedics, because it is a small agency and only one dispatcher is working at any given time. When we take an EMS/first aid call, we get the address only and then transfer the call to our neighboring agency who has more people working. Why? Because while I'm dispatching the police there are other calls coming into me so I can't also dispatch the fire department and dispatch the paramedics and call the ambulance company while answering other calls and the radio. Our neighboring agency has one person to dispatch the fire department (the fire dispatcher), one person to dispatch the paramedics (the police dispatcher), one person to call the ambulance company (a call taker) and they have an extra person (another call taker) to answer any calls that come in to their call center in the meantime. They're a larger municipality so they have more staff. Every agency is different. But back to my next 911 call…it sounded basic to start with. Instead of transferring the call and hanging up, I stayed on the line and listened to the entire call so that I had every possible bit of information, and it was a good thing that I did.

Here's the call:

911: "911, what is the address of your emergency?"

Caller: "123 Main Street."

911: "What is the nature of the emergency?"

Caller: "It's my nephew, his stomach is bleeding I think. He's going to have to go to the hospital."

(I transfer the call to the neighboring agency and I stay on the line listening. If I had not stayed on to listen then I would have sent my officers to 123 Main Street for what sounded like an ulcer problem).

Neighboring 911: "What's wrong with his stomach?"

Caller: "He was stabbed. His crazy ex-girlfriend stabbed him and now she's outside slitting his tires!"

Just by listening for an extra 10 seconds I was able to find out that there was an unstable female on the scene (trespassing) with a knife (criminal possession of a weapon) and she had already stabbed one person (assault) and was now slashing his tires (criminal mischief). That was very important information for my officers to know before they got on the scene, and I was able to share it with them before they arrived only two minutes after I put the call out.

Another call sounded serious to start, but it ended up not being too serious. I also work part-time at a neighboring agency which does dispatch police, fire, and paramedics. While I was working there a man called 911 and said: "I just cut the shit out of myself!" I saw the address on the 911 screen and noticed that he was calling from a restaurant, a pizzeria to be exact. I asked him how this happened and he told me: "I was slicing up a pizza and I slipped, it was an accident," and so I was able to instruct a coworker who was there with him how to cover and elevate the guy's hand until the paramedics and ambulance arrived to take over. It was the caller's panic and shock that made the call sound like maybe he had intentionally sliced his wrist with a kitchen knife, but it only ended up being a pizza cutting accident. You truly never know, so never assume that you do. And always be careful while using a pizza cutter.

Another assumption that all dispatchers are familiar with takes place around the week of Independence Day. So many cities have community events, sometimes even every day of the week, to celebrate the Fourth of July. Many of these events involve a fireworks show and whether fireworks are legal in your State or not a lot of citizens obtain their own fireworks for personal use at home. Fireworks are noisy. When the community is hosting an event that includes fireworks, a lot of the citizens are aware of the celebration and so not too many people will call the police about the noise. When 911 call centers really get busy is the days before and just after July Fourth – with callers reporting hearing gunshots. Fireworks and gunshots do sound very similar. A good way to tell the difference is that a gunshot has a longer echo and makes a deeper thud noise, but most callers aren't able to distinguish this noise from their neighbor on the next block over blowing off fireworks. The callers who report gunshots are frequently adamant that they know the difference between the sound of a gunshot and the sound of fireworks. It does not help that a lot of these calls are not on the actual holiday, because a lot of callers believe that fireworks can only be set off on the holiday. This further convinces the callers that there is no possible way the sound was fireworks so they truly believe that the sound must have been a gunshot. A lot of times the police will respond to the call and find citizens blowing off fireworks. Actually most times that is what they'll encounter. However, this is another one of those times that you don't want to assume that a caller is inaccurate. If you take fifty calls throughout your shift for 'shots fired' around July Fourth and forty-nine of them end up being fireworks, there is still a possibility that the fiftieth call can legitimately be a gunshot call.

Wrong numbers and misdials happen. As a dispatcher, I can't tell you how many butt-dials and purse-dials of 911 I've received over the years. I get offices who have to dial '9' in order to get an outside line and if the number the offices are calling starts with '1-1' then you can guess what happens. Sometimes phones simply have glitches and for whatever reason, 911 is called by seemingly no one. I've received 911 calls and heard toddlers or kids giggling in the background. As a kid, I called 911 just to see what would happen. I reached the 911 operator and then hung up without saying anything to her. Two minutes later there was a police officer at my parents' front door. My father told me I could have been arrested for wasting the police's time and resources and I had plenty of time to think about that because I was sent to my room for the rest of the day. Decades later, children are still curious about what happens if they call 911, except now I'm the one sending the police to check an address after the hang-up. Most agencies have policies in place for 911 calls when no one speaks to the dispatcher, only background noise is heard or when the caller simply hangs up. At my agency, we always send an officer to check the address, even if the caller tells me that they mistakenly dialed 911 and that everything is okay. Why? Because I don't know that the person isn't being forced at gunpoint to tell me that everything is okay. Yes, a lot of times it was a child playing with the phone or a butt-dial or an office clerk's error but you can't ever assume so. At the other agency I work for they also send police if no one speaks to the 911 operator but if the caller stays on the line and can verify the address and name of the business/resident then they won't send an officer. Both agencies attempt to call the number back, though. Sometimes we'll get a parent apologizing profusely, but other times we'll hear yelling and arguing and things being thrown around in the background and no one will answer us. Those are the calls that we listen intently to and gather as much information as we can about the scene just by what we are hearing. We keep the line open and continue to listen until we hear the police on scene to intervene. As a dispatcher, you don't ever want to assume that a 911 call was a prank or a mistake because it could mean someone's life.

Remember that Super Bowl XLIX commercial where a woman calls 911 and when asked what her emergency is, she begins to order a pizza? The camera shows a house with items that have been thrown around, a wall that's been punched and family photos that have been thrown to the floor. The dispatcher asks if the woman knows that she's reached 911 and that it is only for emergencies and she says 'Yes,' and then she asks for cheese and pepperoni so the dispatcher asks her if someone is in the room with her and she says 'Yes,' and so the dispatcher sends the police. That commercial was a great way to remind dispatchers that there can always be something going on that a caller may not be able to verbalize because someone or something on the scene is preventing them to do so. If that dispatcher had assumed that the woman was prank-calling 911 or that she mistakenly dialed 911 to order pizza and he had simply hung up then she would not have received the help that she needed. That's a good dispatcher. Also, dispatchers everywhere were asked by friends and family what 'code words' stood for what trouble was happening. I've been asked by friends: "Does saying 'anchovies' mean that your husband is beating you?" and "Is 'olives' code for a stabbing?" No, there is not a universal list of pizza toppings that callers use as code words to secretly describe a situation. Dispatchers do not go to special 'Pizza Topping Secret Codes' training of any sort. We're simply taught to listen. We are trained to be aware that there could be important information that the caller may not be able to tell us out of fear of someone else in the house with them. That's a good time to ask the caller 'Yes' or 'No' questions because then it sounds to someone else as if the caller could be talking to anyone and not 911. Verbal pizza orders aren't the only way callers ask for help. In Florida a woman placed a pizza order online and in the delivery instructions portion of her order she typed 'Please help. Get 911 to me,' and also wrote '911hostagehelp!' in the order. The pizza restaurant knew this woman was a regular customer and because she'd never done anything like this they did as the instructions asked and called the police. As it turns out, her boyfriend was holding her and her children hostage with a knife. He had no idea she had summoned help by ordering a pizza online. If you're ever contacted by a restaurant that delivers pizza or other food and they ask for the police for a customer then you likely will not have a wealth of information. You'll have an address and possibly a name or phone number of the customer, but probably not much more. You can put the call out to officers exactly as you've received it. Maybe a supervisor will ask you to call the phone number that the customer provided the restaurant in order to attempt to get more information, but most likely you will not be asked to do this. Someone who places an online pizza order to ask for police likely can't talk on the phone to give further information about what's going on at that address. Of course, you don't want to assume that is the case, but let someone else make that call. What you can do is perform a quick search of the history of the address. Maybe you'll find that there have been a lot of domestic calls there, or that one of the residents has a restraining order against someone who isn't allowed to be at that address, or that someone at that address has a weapon permit or an arrest warrant. That information would be helpful to your officers because it will give them a better idea what they're walking in to.

Chapter Seven – Who Goes Where?

How do you know which officer to send to a call? Most agencies have 'beats' or areas that an officer patrols. The officer generally stays in his area or 'beat' but will sometimes go to another 'beat' if he's backing up another officer on a traffic stop or a complaint. A lot of agencies have two or more main roads in their jurisdiction. Imagine Main Street runs north to south and Center Street runs east to west. A good way to divide that up would for one officer to cover all of the northwest (everything north of Main Street and west of Center Street), another to cover the northeast (everything north of Center Street and East of Center Street), another to cover the southwest (everything south of Main Street and west of Center Street) and a final officer to cover the southeast (everything South of Main Street and east of Center Street). Some agencies have computer programs that prompt you which area a call is in once you begin to type the address, and some programs will also list 'Officer X' is who should respond to that call.

At my agency, we send two cars/two patrols to each call but it is typically up to the officers whether or not the 'backup' patrol or 'sidecar' actually responds. For a violent fight at a bar: of course, the second officer will respond, and so would one or two other officers if they're free – even officers from neighboring jurisdictions will respond to help if they hear the call put out over the radio. But for a little old lady who called 911 because she can't find her cat in the house: just one officer would probably be able to handle that on his own. But what if a call comes in for the Northeast officer and he's on a traffic stop or on another call? Then I'd send the Northwest patrol. Most agencies have an alternate officer that they want to be sent to a call if the primary officer is tied up with something.

Sometimes an agency will get a very serious call that ties up all of their officers. It could be an unstable person making suicidal threats, holed up in the house with a firearm with their family members as hostages. What happens if someone on the other side of the town calls 911 and needs the police right away too, but you are all out of officers to send because they're all outside of the unstable person's house? Most agencies have a policy in place for such instances. At my agency, the officer in charge will tell me to call our neighboring jurisdiction to ask their superior officer if their officers can cover our calls. Yes, police agencies do this a lot. Sure if it's the old lady from before who can't find her cat in the house then the call can sit for a while, but if it's at all a serious call then we need to send someone, even if that officer is from another agency. Find out your agency's policy or procedure on this, because you don't want to be calling your Captain or Chief's cell phone to find out what to do when he's sitting underneath a window in some bushes in case the unstable person runs out the back door with a gun in hand. That ringing cell phone would give away his position. Your department may have a SWAT team or squad too that could respond to the unstable person's house and free up a few of your officers.

Chapter Eight – Check the History

When I put a call out over the radio, I've already clicked a little button on my computer that says 'history' if I'm not familiar with the address's history of complaints. By clicking that button I can see all of the calls that our agency has ever had at that particular address no matter who has lived there.

When I was a kid I called 911 to see what would happen; the police showed up at my house and I was then grounded by my parents. If I were to put my childhood home address into the computer, there would be a 'welfare check' or a '911 hang-up' call in the history even though it was decades ago.

As much trouble as I was in with my parents (and the police) for unnecessarily tying up valuable resources, an officer could be in much more trouble if he isn't familiar with a particular address or the people who live at or frequent that address. An officer may be responding to an address because someone who was walking past the house found a loose dog. Normally the officer might secure the dog in his car until the owner can be located, or I might call animal control to collect the dog from our officer if animal control is on duty. But what about the address itself? What if the resident is heavily anti-police and says so on social media? What if the resident has posted photos of himself holding firearms online with captions such as: "Cop Killer" on the photos? What if that resident is home and happens to see a police officer outside of his house once the passerby and animal control are gone? What might happen?

What could happen is the anti-police resident could come rushing out of his house with an assault rifle and shoot the officer who is stationary in his vehicle. But I have clicked the 'history' button and I know all about the resident at that address, and I've already told the three officers responding all about it before they have even arrived on scene to find a very confused-looking passerby who is probably wondering why three police officers have shown up for one lost dog. Social media is monitored, heavily, by law enforcement agencies. If we don't see a suspicious post like the one mentioned here, someone else has and you better believe that we get tips on this sort of person and behavior all the time. We can attach a warning both to the address and to a person so that any time either is queried or entered we'll see that warning and pass it along to the responding officers so they know what they can potentially be dealing with.

Checking the history, warnings or memos associated with a person or an address is invaluable but not just in cases where violence is possible. Sometimes the police are called for medical help because an elderly male inside fell and he can't get to the door to unlock it. Sure in the movies they just use a battering ram and bust the door open, or the fire department axes the door into shreds. But you can't do that to a little old man who has fallen and broken a hip. How will he replace the door? This is where we enter the locations of hidden keys or lockbox codes. We never give them out over the radio for security reasons, but this is yet another thing to check for before the officers arrive on the scene to help someone. You need to help the officers so they can help the callers.

Checking the history is good for other types of calls as well. Maybe it is the middle of the night and we get a commercial burglary alarm at one of our schools. Checking the history, I'd likely be able to find out who we've contacted in the past to let us into the school after-hours in order to conduct a walk-through. That information would be helpful in any type of alarm call whether at a school, gas station, law office, or really any other type of structure.

I also check the history for domestic calls. Officers are required to fill out domestic incident reports or DIRs and I know that once of those check-boxes asks if either of the parties have any sort of restraining orders against the other. If there is a restraining order in effect and it was violated: then someone is getting arrested. By taking an extra ten seconds to check the history at that address I can determine if there are any restraining orders and that helps the officers with not only their paperwork but with facilitating an arrest if need be. It saves them time.

Over time you'll become familiar with not only your 'frequent fliers' but also with addresses that your police officers routinely get called to whether it is for landlord/tenant dispute, loud music complaints, ongoing neighbor disputes or potential drug dealing. If your agency has a way for you to check the history of an address then I suggest that you review it for each and every call so that you are aware of any potentially dangerous activity or people at that address and so that you can pass that information over to your officers before they arrive on the scene.

Chapter Nine –

Silent Dispatches and Other Means of Communication

There comes a time when certain things cannot or should not be said over the police radio. If a dispatcher says on the radio: 'All patrols, silent dispatch,' that means that whatever is going on is not for the public to hear.

Thanks to technology a person does not even need to purchase a police scanner to hear what is going on in their neighborhoods, there is an app for that or a website for that, for free! If a resident sees the fire department rush by their house with lights & sirens activated, they can open the app or the site and listen to find out in just minutes that their neighbor burned their morning toast. This would potentially save a dispatcher from yet another phone call from that same resident asking: "Why is the fire department at my neighbor's house?" when the dispatcher on duty is on another phone call instructing someone how to perform CPR on an unrelated 911 call.

There are instances where that easily audible information can work against the police too, though. If you are a drug dealer with lots of illegal drugs in your house and you heard this: "All patrols, 123 Main Street for a drug deal in progress with suspected firearms inside the house, called in by Mrs. Smith across the street," then you may not be very happy. You might try to get rid of the drugs, or you may later retaliate against Mrs. Smith for turning you in. But we as dispatchers are always mindful of what we put out over the radio because we know that it isn't only our officers listening. We as dispatchers do not give drug dealers a head start to the bathroom to flush their supply, we as dispatchers do not put neighbors in danger of retaliation. We simply say 'Silent dispatch' and then alert our officers in other ways about what is going on at that address. We have cell phones, computer chats and more to communicate with our officers.

There are other times where a dispatcher may not put information out over the radio. Once one of my officers found an open front door at a local business, it was about two in the morning and he knew from his regular patrolling that the business should have been locked hours ago. It was a pizza place. Because he called out with an open door, I send a second officer to back him up and then I checked the history for a key holder because someone has to lock the door to the pizza place. There was a lot of valuable equipment in there that needed to be secured. The key holder ended up being the owner, who was in a weeks-long argument with the co-owner, his brother, who was the last one to leave and had apparently been the one who neglected to lock the door. The key holder told me to call his brother to lock the door since he was the one who left it open, and so I did. The brother was furious because he had just fallen asleep and I had woken him up. He was also mad because his brother (who lived closer to the restaurant) was refusing to respond to lock the place up. The second brother told me that if his brother didn't care that the place was open then he didn't either. I called the primary officer on the scene, on his work cell phone, and gave him the information. I did not get on the radio and say: "Both key holders do not care that the pizza place at 123 Main Street is wide open until morning" because if someone other than the police were listening that they would know that the pizza place is wide open all night long. I would have basically been saying: "Need a pizza cutter? A cash register? Some tables and chairs? Someplace to do drugs tonight? Go to the pizza place, no one is watching it until morning and it is wide open!"

Aside from sensitive information like drugs houses, unsecured buildings and hidden keys or codes, there are certain things that you should never say over the police radio. Profanity is an obvious no-no, but terminology matters too. A white muscle shirt is sometimes referred to as 'wife beater' in civilian life but that is not something you want to say over a police radio because it is entirely unprofessional not to mention insensitive.

Not all motorcycles are Harley Davidsons, some are smaller and sportier bikes which I would call a 'sports motorcycle' and not a 'crotch rocket' over the radio. Always be mindful of what you're saying over the radio because you do not know who is listening at any given time. Using profanity, slang, or potentially offensive language will not go over well for you or for your department; always keep it professional.

Part 3 – Jurisdiction Knowledge and the Public

Chapter Ten – Know Your Jurisdiction

Fun fact about my agency's borders: if you're walking and you slip in the street on West Street, then we respond to help you up. If you slip on the sidewalk on the west side of the road, then another agency responds to help you. Yep: the street is our jurisdiction, the curb and the sidewalk is the other agency's jurisdiction. And just one street south of that is a third agency's jurisdiction!

On North Street, the numerical addresses are either even or odd just like any other street. The houses on the south side of the street (the odd-numbered ones) are our jurisdiction, as is the whole street itself but the houses on the north side of the street (even numbered) are another agency's jurisdiction. Since both municipalities forbid overnight parking on the streets during the winter time, new police officers tend to get confused about whether or not they can issue a parking ticket for cars parked on that street because they're not sure if they are in their own jurisdiction or not.

We have a car dealership that takes up two blocks one of our main roads. The lot that sells trucks and cars is our neighboring agency's jurisdiction while the service & maintenance center is our jurisdiction. If someone doesn't return a loaner car to the maintenance center then my agency completes a stolen vehicle report, but if someone doesn't return from a test drive from the sales lot then the neighboring agency responds to do the stolen vehicle report.

On East Street, the addresses from one to four hundred are our jurisdiction, but addresses over four hundred are another jurisdiction's.

On South Street, we have jurisdiction only on the odd-numbered addresses, and only from nine hundred and one to eighteen hundred and one – the even-numbered address from nine hundred to eighteen hundred and two are handled by the agency to the south of us; the middle of the street is the border. On South Street still: numbers up to nine hundred and higher than eighteen hundred are handled by the agency to the north of us.

We have one road in my area that goes through two whole counties and that includes many towns in between the road's starting point and ending point. If there is an accident on that road then a dispatcher needs to first ask in what town the accident occurred and then on which side of the street, because the exact location is what determines which police agency responds. To add to the 'fun' of this, none of the intersecting side streets share a name or even a directional hint. It would be nice if the intersecting roads were named 'West ____' on the west side of this long road and 'East ____' on the east side of this long road but we have no such luck. Completely unrelated street names are what we have to work with. Coconut Street could be west of the long road and Mayor's Parkway could be east of the long road, even when both streets are essentially a continuation of the each other.

Aside from memorizing your own jurisdiction, it is helpful to also get to know which roads connect your jurisdiction to other jurisdictions and which streets in those jurisdictions are close to your jurisdiction. Why? Because if the agency to the south of you is pursuing a vehicle in a high-speed chase on Main Street and the vehicle is heading north then your officers are going to want to know that information so they can assist the agency or try to apprehend the vehicle and driver. Same with the agency to the north of us – if a drunk driver is heading south down Main Street then I know it's coming our way and I'll alert my officers. If another agency calls you at two in the morning and says: "Hey we found a bunch of cars with the dome lights on the inside of them on Any Street. We don't have any sightings on suspects but we just thought we'd let you know," then you better know that Any Street is only three streets out of your jurisdiction and that you need to tell your officers that someone is going through people's unlocked cars and taking things in the area because it is likely that your jurisdiction's residents will also be victims of petit larceny and your officers may come across those responsible for committing those larcenies!

Remember: people do not always know where they live (more on this in the next chapter) so it will be up to you to determine whether or not your agency responds or if another agency responds. By knowing your jurisdiction you'll be better able to access where help is needed.

Not only do you need to know your own jurisdiction and parts of the jurisdictions surrounding yours but you also have to know which officer to send to which areas or streets. When I first started I made a typed list of every street in our jurisdiction and which patrol officer was assigned to that street or 'beat' so that I would know right away who to send. Over time it will become automatic for you, but do I still refer to that list occasionally because my agency only covers odd numbers of certain streets and even numbers of other streets and so on.

It is vital that you memorize your jurisdiction and at least the closest areas of your neighboring jurisdictions.

Chapter Eleven –

The Public Doesn't Know Where They Actually Live

The public does not always know where actually live. I don't say this to be mean, I say it because their confusion about this occurs on a daily basis. Think of your own town: how many zip codes are there? How many police departments are there in a ten-mile area? Do your neighborhoods have nicknames?

In my area, one of the local suburbs has an official name of 'A' (which I just made up). Within 'A' there are some pretty ritzy houses and neighborhoods that I'll call 'Glam-ville' and 'Mansion-ville.' Within the town of 'A', there is also a neighborhood with housing that used to be strictly for somewhat-independent mentally challenged people in the 1960's and is now affordable housing. That neighborhood kept the 1960's name of 'Crazy Town' however inappropriate it is by today's standards. If anyone in Glam-ville, Mansion-ville or Crazy Town called the police: the 'A' town police would respond. There is no Glam-ville Police Department or Crazy Town Police Department. In other words, there are different neighborhoods with different nicknames but they all happen to fall in just one police jurisdiction.

The issue that the public has is when zip codes or the name of a place comes into play. Let's say Glam-ville has a zip code of 12345 and the mailing address for a street looks like this: 123 Main Street, Town of 'A' NY, 12345. Someone still in Glam-ville, and still living in town 'A' might have a different mailing address such as 456 Main Street, Town of 'B' NY, 12345. So while the mailing address and zip code indicate that the person lives in the town of 'B' they actually live in the town of 'A.' Surely there are similar instances in your town, city or village.

It doesn't get any less confusing when places are named after streets or towns! There is an apartment building on North Street, called the 'North Apartments' which is in the city of 'South.' Those residents call the North Police Department for help, insisting that they live in North because their apartments are on North Street and called the North Apartments. But the correct responding agency is the South Police Department.

A lot of people don't work in their own neighborhoods either. They might live in the town of 'C' but work in the town of 'E.' If they call 911 on the way to work to report a car accident they might tell the dispatcher that the accident is in the town of 'D,' when it's actually in the town of 'E' but the caller isn't familiar enough with the area to know the difference because he just commutes through it.

At my agency there are a handful of officers who live thirty miles away from the station, the rest of us live pretty close by. Those of us who live close by tend to know a bit more about our own neighborhoods, so we're a little more familiar with the areas surrounding our municipality. As a dispatcher I can easily tell a caller that the street he is calling from is another jurisdiction, but if I commuted thirty miles to work and worked in a large call center (and was only familiar with the route that I drive to work) then I might have a hard time figuring out exactly which police department to send to that person. Side streets, nicknames for neighborhoods and different zip codes might throw me off otherwise; this is why a lot of municipalities require that their employees live within the municipality that they work for – because they're familiar with it.

Cell phones complicate things further! I mentioned that when a call comes into 911 from a landline then the address of the call displays on the screen. If the call is from a cell phone then the address of the closest cell phone tower shows on the screen. What I didn't mention is that some cities have one giant call center that takes ALL cell phone calls and then transfers them to the appropriate agencies. Don't worry – it only takes a few extra seconds to transfer calls to the correct agency, and not every area is set up in the same manner as my area. If you have a choice to call 911 from a cell phone or from a landline: pick the landline!

As a dispatcher: know your area, know your surrounding areas, know the neighborhoods and know their nicknames and zip codes. A great way to do this is to go on a Ride Along with an officer or two. During my training at both agencies that I work for I was required to do a Ride Along and there were areas & places in my own neighborhood that I had no idea even existed!

Chapter Twelve – 'Frequent Fliers'

What is a frequent flier? A frequent flier is a person who calls 911 or your non-emergency number for anything and everything. Very rarely is a police response required when one of our frequent fliers calls the station, but remember: don't assume anything!

We have a few frequent fliers in our jurisdiction. One woman, let's call her 'Pauline,' calls to complain about music being played at deafening volumes – except no one can hear it but Pauline. Pauline will call five or six times a day for a few months in a row and then she won't call again for a month or so. We also have Rob, an independent but semi-mentally challenged man who really admires police officers. Really, he idolizes them. He wears a 'security' jacket and walks around in town to look for 'the bad guys.' Rob likes to call the police station to report suspicious people or occurrences because he wants to be 'one of the good guys' as he says, but none of these calls to date have yielded any arrests. Rob also takes it upon himself to direct traffic on side streets even if there is none. We also have a 'Joanne' who is elderly and has no family in the area. She calls the station to insist that her car or purse were stolen, even if she is in her car and holding her purse. Then there is 'Jim' who lives below 'Joe' and they both call to tattle on the other. Jim's favorite complaint? That Joe is smoking a cigarette upstairs and that Jim can't sleep because of it. Joe likes to call and demand that Jim be arrested for harassing him, 'harassing' being Jim asking Joe to turn down his television's volume.

A lot of times if a person continues to call the police and the complaint is unfounded, a police agency will do a referral. That may mean a phone call to Adult Services or a similar agency. We want to make sure that if that person cannot safely care for himself or herself, or if their mind isn't what it used to be, then they are given the help that they need. Sure today Joanne may be certain that her car was stolen, even though the officer will plainly see it parked in her locked garage – but tomorrow Joanne may cook something on the stove before bed and she may be 'certain' that she turned off the stove when in fact she will not have, causing a fire or carbon monoxide poisoning.

Each frequent flier is different with their needs and with their abilities to cope with day to day life. As a dispatcher it is not your job to judge them – your job is to get the information, even if it seems ridiculous, and then send an officer. It is common sense: if someone is calling and asking for the police, then you send the police.

People with mental health issues can truly believe that their home is being broken into even if no one is there. It is real to them and they feel very real fear, so do not judge a person because to that person they are in a life-or-death situation. A little bit of compassion goes a long way for these people, so be nice to them when they call you even if it is the fourth time in two hours.

Part 4 – Be Informed and Be Aware

Chapter Thirteen – Be Informed

I have a routine that sets me apart from other dispatchers and it is not difficult to do: when I start my shift I look at all of the call activity that has occurred since my last shift. I do this because I like to be informed of all that has happened.

If four hours before my shift a vehicle was repossessed but the owner wasn't aware of the repossession: the vehicle's owner may call during my shift to report their car being stolen. I don't want to send an officer to the person's house only for the officer to run the person's license plate and find out it was repossessed and the repo agency did report it as repossessed to our agency just four hours ago. It is senseless and it is a waste of the officer's time.

This is incredibly helpful in saving the dispatcher's time as well, especially in the event of referrals to public utilities or other agencies. Just today an officer called in over the radio to inform me that all of the street lights on a particular street were out and he asked me to notify the electric company so they could look into it and fix the issue. Because I had already read the previous shift's activity I knew that the officer on the last shift and the same beat had already notified the dispatcher who was working before me to call the electric company about the same street lights. That saved me a phone call! Personally, I'd feel that both I and the department would seem a bit stupid calling the electric company twice in nine hours to report the same issue; it would seem that we do not communicate with each other within our department, and I don't want the department looking bad. The department has a briefing before each shift where they pass on important information but street lights being out isn't high on their discussion list.

If you have access to your agency's police reports (not all dispatchers do; at times only higher-seniority dispatchers have permission to do so while newer dispatchers do not) then I suggest that you view them if you're permitted to do so. I can't tell you how many times I've worked when one of our officers comes across someone out in the field and the person is wanted for a crime that occurred earlier in the day or week. It could be an assault, a shoplifting incident, or a hit & run suspect. Odds are I will hear the name on the radio, I will sense a familiarity and check the police reports and complaints for the person's name. If I run a person's driver's license in my state then I'll see whether or not their license is valid, what type of license they have as well as their address and height and eye color. If the person has a warrant or a restraining order then that will show up as well. But what won't show up is all of the contacts that person has had with our agency or with other agencies – so by regularly reading the past reports and complaints I'm more likely to know if a person is a suspect of a crime or even just someone that we're looking for or another agency may be looking for.

Once I was working back-to-back shifts and during the first half, an agency about thirty miles away announced a 'silver alert' to the rest of the county. A silver alert is when a senior citizen has gone missing, usually the senior has dementia or is otherwise incapable of 100% self-care. Silver alert subjects sometimes leave a senior or assisted living home and then a short time later become disoriented and get lost. Other times they simply wander off. The first half of my shift that day went pretty quickly and before I knew it the day shift police officers had left and the afternoon shift officers were in. An hour before the end of my sixteen hour day one of my officers called out with a man who was sitting on a bench outside of an apartment building. When he gave me the man's name over the radio I was very surprised to learn that the man he had come across was the same missing senior from the silver alert! As it turned out, the man used to live in the apartments that he was outside of, and he had somehow traveled thirty miles over about ten hours without money or a vehicle. The man did have dementia and could not remember how he had managed to travel so far without the means to do so, but we did get him back home. If I had not worked a double shift I still would have known that the silver alert was in effect because I would have checked all of the call activity that occurred since I last worked. I would have seen the agency had notified the county of the silver alert. When the officer asked over the radio: "Dispatch, see if anyone may be looking for this subject or if anyone reported him missing," I was able to instantly answer: "That's affirmative, a silver alert was issued from the Town of C ten hours ago, I've advised them we have him and they're sending a car to meet you halfway if you're clear to transport him." That's being informed and it is also taking initiative by anticipating what the police officer needs to know to do his job.

Chapter Fourteen – Be Aware: Listen Up!

Once I worked at a national retail store for some extra holiday cash. When I applied and later accepted the job the condition was that I was a 'part-time' and a 'seasonal' employee, meaning I was not interested in full-time employment and the company would essentially be laying me off after the holiday season. This was a clothing store that had about four locations in my area; I was scheduled to either work the cash register or man the fitting rooms. When I did not have customers at the register or in the fitting room I'd return discarded fitting room clothing to the racks or shelves, I'd go to the tables and refold all of the t-shirts, I'd sweep the fitting room or clean the window at the front of the store. Of all four stores, they had hired about one hundred extra workers and anticipated hiring two of those extra workers full-time. After the season was over I was asked to stay on as a full-time employee, with the possibility of management. I turned them down but did ask why they had approached me with the proposition since I had indicated I was only interested in part-time and seasonal work. Their answer? I kept busy & productive whereas other hires had simply stood around waiting for work to happen. Why am I telling you about my one-time retail job? Because I went the extra mile, and that work ethic can translate into any profession.

Dispatchers sit in one room or call center where they sometimes have very quiet days with minimal calls coming in and nothing happening out on the road. Trying to keep mentally stimulated for eight hours or more can be tough, therefore many dispatchers try to occupy their time between calls with something to keep them alert. Some dispatchers read, some play games on tablets and some even do squats and lunges at their desks. I know a couple of dispatchers who knit on the job too. Depending on the agency there may be a television available to use too, or a dispatcher might log into his Netflix account and catch up on his favorite shows.

What do I do to occupy my time in between calls? I listen to our neighboring police agencies' radio. Not very exciting at times, but very helpful. I know my agency's borders inside and out, and I know our two neighboring agencies' main streets and side streets too. If I hear about a fire going on to the south of my agency I notify my officers because odds are the smoke will come into our jurisdiction and my officers will go looking for a fire in our jurisdiction if I don't tell them that there is a confirmed fire in our neighboring jurisdiction. If the agency to the north of us has a drunk driver heading southbound then I'll know to alert my officers of the make and model of the vehicle so they can keep an eye out for it as well in case the vehicle enters our jurisdiction. I'll even run the plate if I've got it in order to give my officers an idea of where that drunk driver may be headed. I've heard officers on the radio from other agencies asking their dispatchers to call my agency and see if we can send one of our officers to an address in our jurisdiction to look for a person. It can be a teenager who didn't come home from a friend's house and her parents cannot get a hold of her on her cell phone, it can be the ex-boyfriend of a woman who assaulted her current boyfriend in the neighboring jurisdiction but resides in our jurisdiction and is believed to be back at home, or it can be that there was a death of person in another jurisdiction and the family in our jurisdiction needs to notified.

I listen to have a head's up on things that may be coming our way but I listen to possibly prevent crimes in our own jurisdiction. Once I heard that a convenience store in the jurisdiction south to ours was robbed. I jotted down the description of the suspect as well as the make and model of the vehicle he had driven away in, which happened to be northbound on a road that connects their jurisdiction to ours. About fifteen minutes later another convenience store in that jurisdiction was robbed; all of the suspect and vehicle information was identical to the previous robbery and the suspect was still northbound. I shared what I had heard with my officers and they kept extra watches on our convenience stores for the remainder of the shift. No robberies occurred in our jurisdiction that day. Sure it could be that the robber went home or maybe went out for a night on the town with his stolen money, but he could have also seen a police car parked at the convenience store and thought better of committing a third robbery. Listening to your neighboring jurisdictions' radio keeps you in the know for incidents that could spill over into your jurisdiction.

Part 5 – The Police Language

Chapter Fifteen– 'Radio Ear' and Learning the Lexicon

'Radio ear' is a phrase that refers to a dispatcher's ability to listen to what is being said on their radio. Hearing an officer call on-scene at a location is easy if there isn't any static and there isn't anything else going on at the moment. But if you're on the phone while he's transmitting over the radio: will you be able to hear both what your officer is saying and what your caller is saying? Will you still be able to make out what he's saying if another officer calls in on a different frequency at the same time to ask you to run a license plate for him? What if you're on the phone while those two officers are calling in at the same time? Being able to hear and understand several things at once is called having a good 'radio ear.' Being at work and experiencing this is one way to develop your own radio ear but there are other methods that you can practice in real life that can help you to accomplish this.

If your agency permits it, you can take home a scanner and simply listen to the transmissions during your free time. That's also a helpful way to get to know your officers' voices if you're brand new. If borrowing a police scanner isn't permitted then go online and search for police frequencies to listen to and listen live to any agency's transmissions just to get an idea how several different communications can happen all at once. There are even apps for this sort of thing that you can download to your phone for free. Try to listen to two different agencies at once; one on your computer or tablet and one on your phone. See if you can mentally keep track of who is saying what.

You can practice developing your radio ear in real life too. If you have children and have ever had to make an important phone call, you'll know exactly what I mean. You're trying to listen to the person on the phone and your kids (who have probably been quiet most of the day) suddenly feel the need to talk to you while you're on the phone. Hearing and understanding the person on the phone while simultaneously figuring out what your kids are saying is a great way to develop your radio ear. So is watching two television channels at one time. You can even go out to a restaurant and try to eavesdrop on the conversation at the table next to yours while you hold your own conversation with your spouse or friend. You can do the same on public transportation, at sporting events or just about anywhere else that there are people.

Police dispatching also requires a dispatcher to learn phonetic alphabets, sets of codes, and a lot of terms that aren't common in everyday life for civilians. The purpose of this way of speaking is to clarify information and to reduce radio time. In this day and age with the technology that is available to all of us, citizens can easily listen to police radio transmissions by a scanner, online or through an app and the public may not understand certain codes (and that can be a good thing).

When police radio into dispatch with a license plate number or a person's name they'll often say what they see or hear and then spell it out phonetically. That's because so many letters sound similar, especially over a radio. 'B' sounds like 'C,' 'D,' 'E,' 'G' and 'Z.' 'F' sounds like 'S.' Therefore an officer may call out a plate as: 'ABC123,' and then say: 'Alpha, Bravo, Charlie, 123,' or 'Adam, Boy, Charles, 123.' They'll do the same when asking for a warrant check: they'll say the person's name and then spell it phonetically such as 'Smith, that's Sam, Mary, Ida, Tom, Henry' or 'Sierra, Mike, India, Tango,

Hotel.' It is important that you hear the correct letters corresponding with license plate checks because if you were to enter it wrong in the computer then you could end up missing that a particular car was reported stolen, or a person with a warrant might be let go because you misheard the spelling.

Here is a list of two different versions of phonetic alphabets:

Adam	Alpha
Boy	Bravo
Charles	Charlie
David	Delta
Edward	Echo
Frank	Foxtrot
George	Golf
Henry	Hotel
Ida	India
John	Juliet
King	Kilo
Lincoln	Lima
Mary	Mike
Nora	November
Ocean	Oscar
Paul	Papa
Queen	Quebec
Robert	Romeo
Sam	Sierra

Union	Uniform
Victor	Victor
William	Whiskey
X-ray	X-ray
Yellow	Yankee
Zebra	Zulu

The list on the right is the NATO phonetic alphabet and is the most commonly used in the police communication world. If I am relaying a license plate to an officer over the radio, I'll use the list on the right because a lot of my officers are ex-military and since the military uses the NATO phonetic alphabet then that's the one the officers are usually more familiar with. If the member of the public is on the phone giving me a license plate number and I want to repeat it back to that caller for clarity then I'll use the list on the left. Sometimes callers get snagged up on 'kilo' or 'foxtrot' because they may not know how to spell 'kilo' or they think that 'foxtrot' is two words and that I'm giving them an extra letter ('T') that isn't in there. I suggest learning both of the phonetic alphabets and using whichever your agency prefers or, if allowed, whichever version you're more comfortable with. When you're first starting out it doesn't hurt to print out a list and keep it nearby, otherwise you'll do what I did when I was a brand new dispatcher: you'll resort to using letters of just about anything (elephant, saxophone, paperclip, etc.) which can be rather embarrassing to do.

Police officers also have codes for communicating a variety of things. There is a widely-used system for these codes and that is called 'The 10 Codes,' where the number '10' is said which signifies that the next number is the code, such as '4.' I think anyone who has seen an old police movie or television show knows that '10-4' means 'okay' or 'understood.' Every agency is different; in my county, one police agency uses plain speak, two police agencies use another set of codes, one agency uses their own codes and some agencies use the 10-codes.

No matter which set of codes an agency uses, there are many uses for the codes. Officers have a code for calling out on a traffic stop, asking for a warrant check, calling on-scene at a call and clearing from a call. They have codes for prisoner transports, beginning and ending their tour, returning to headquarters, asking for another officer's location and more.

You're probably familiar with the word 'DWI' and I'm sure you know that it means 'driving while intoxicated.' How about 'GOA'? That means 'gone on arrival.' There is D&D (drunk and disorderly), NOK (next of kin) BOLO (be on lookout), ATL (attempt to locate) WINQ (warrant inquiry), LS (last seen) B&E (breaking and entering), FTA (failure to appear), APB (all-points bulletin) and many more. Police agencies use these abbreviations to communicate within the department and with other agencies. 'F' is used for 'female,' 'M' is used for male, 'U' is used for 'unknown' when describing a person's sex. For the race, it is 'A' for 'Asian,' 'W' for 'White,' 'B' for 'Black,' and 'H' for 'Hispanic'. For directions of travel, it is 'N/B' for 'northbound' and so on.

If you're on duty and a message comes across your computer such as: "ATL – W/F driving E/B on Main Street from the Walmart in a black Ford pickup, stole three blenders, LSW a pink shirt and blue jeans" then you'd know that a white female last seen wearing a pink shirt and blue jeans is driving eastbound and that the agency wants her located because she is going to be charged with petit larceny for stealing three blenders. She'll also likely be charged with criminal possession of stolen property. Alternatively, 'ATL' could have been substituted with 'BOLO' or 'APB'.

If you watch any police/crime drama television show and a character on the show goes missing, you may hear the detectives on the show saying: "Put out an APB for him," which would mean that a message (bulletin) would be sent to every police agency (all points) with the missing character's information so that he can hopefully be located.

Between two different phonetic alphabets, abbreviations, acronyms, and codes there is a lot to learn when it comes to the police lexicon; it truly seems like a whole other language! Just keep in mind that the public is not going to be familiar with these terms. If someone calls to find out if the police are on the way yet after their initial call for help and you tell them that the officers 'have been dispatched,' that may not be understood to mean 'on the way' to your caller. 'On scene' to you means just that, but to a caller 'the police are there now' makes more sense.

Part 6 – Working with Police Officers
Chapter Sixteen – Officer Safety

It is imperative that you know where all of your officers are, always. Yes, you will send them directly to a lot of calls that came in on 911 so you'll know exactly where they are going, but officers also do a lot of self-initiated work out there on the road. They pull cars over for traffic violations, they notice something out of the ordinary like a business's lights being on past a certain time, and they get flagged down by people on the road. Your job is to know where each and every one of them is at all times – whether it is on patrol, transporting a prisoner to another agency or location, out on a traffic stop or even in the restroom for a minute (yes, that is important information too because you don't want to send someone to a life-or-death call when that person isn't actually available to respond!)

Why is it so important to know where every officer is all of the time? Because in the event that they need police back-up or any sort of medical assistance then you need to know where to send those additional resources.

A test I like to give my trainees once I have them answering the radio is to arrange ahead of time with an officer that he calls out over the radio to dispatch with something minor, but in an area where I know that his portable radio will have some static covering his voice. Every agency has these 'blind spots' where you may have to ask an officer to repeat what he's said due to a bit of static covering his transmission. Trainees are typically afraid to ask an officer to repeat himself, thinking that the officer will assume that the trainee is not listening to him and that the trainee is not doing his job when really this is a test to make sure that the trainee places the officer's safety over his own perceived negligence. The first time this test is conducted the trainees all simply say 'ok you're on location' or whatever terminology or code your agency uses to convey that you're understood the radio transmission. I will then ask the trainees: "Where is he?" and they all say: "I don't know, there was static covering him," and that's when I ask them: "What if he's with someone who shoots him – where will you send help? Would you rather feel a bit embarrassed to ask him to repeat himself or would you rather he gets hurt or worse?" Lesson learned! Even if the incident the officer calls in is minor, perhaps he found a lost kitten, you never know who may approach him out there and whether or not that person has a hate for police or is upset they received a ticket or has a weapon. Always know where your officers are so that you know where to send help if they need it.

Yes, some officers will be irritated that they have to repeat information, sometimes more than once, but they know that you need the correct information for safety's sake. If an officer is spelling out a person's name for a warrant check over the radio a lot of letters can sound alike. 'D' sounds like 'E' and 'B' and 'C' and 'F' sounds like 'S.' That's why officers will often say a name, such as 'Smith' and then spell it out phonetically as 'Sam, Mary, Ida, Tom, Henry' or 'Sierra, Mike, India, Tango, Hotel.' If you hear the wrong letters or name and then enter the wrong name into the system to check for a warrant then you could be giving the officer inaccurate information. That would be one lucky day for the warrant suspect if he actually has a warrant and gets to walk away because you made a mistake or didn't want to ask the officer to repeat the information. And if you don't know where your officer is when he's requesting that warrant check and the warrant suspect decides to flee, then you'll want to know what area to send back-up to help with apprehending the suspect.

Most times if an officer pulls a driver over for a traffic infraction such as driving at nighttime without headlights – another officer stops to check on them. Even officers from neighboring jurisdictions will stop to make sure everything in on the up & up – cops have each other's backs whether or not they work for the same agency or for different agencies. If my officer is on a traffic stop for nine minutes without an officer checking on him at all: I ask him over the radio if he's all set. Sure maybe the person is driving a rental car with manual headlights whereas his regular car has automatic headlights and maybe my officer is helping the driver figure out how to turn on the headlights. But it is also possible that the driver is a drug dealer who has a large amount of heroin and cocaine in the car and does not want to go to jail so he's going to shoot the officer who pulls him over for driving with no headlights.

Officers call things out over the radio, too. Maybe an officer is driving and spots someone down on the ground and after checking on the person he determines that the person needs first aid. As long as you know where that officer is, you can give a good location to medical personnel so they can help that person.

Chases are another time that you'll want to know where your officers are. Whether it is a high-speed chase in a vehicle or a foot chase through backyards – if the chase ends up with a struggle you need to know where to send help if there is an officer in trouble. Knowing where his fellow officers are even if they're not involved with the chase is helpful too because you'll know which officer is closest to the officer in trouble. Some agencies have computer programs that display the locations of their fleet which updates on a constant basis which is incredibly helpful.

It is also important to know who the officer is with and also who they can potentially be exposed to. An officer out on a call may very well have a backup officer on the scene with him but what about other people? Let's say a woman called 911 to report being scammed out of money online. That would seem to be a pretty routine call with little possibility for danger, right? You'd think that the police would arrive at her house to advise her what to do about her dilemma and that would be it. But 'routine' calls don't always play out that way. As the dispatcher, you've got to think on your feet and try to be one step ahead of the game, even for 'routine' calls. Let's say that you've taken the 911 call from the scammed woman so you have her name and the address that officers were requested at. When you're generating a complaint in the computer, you notice that she's already on file in the system but at a different address. You perform a quick search to check her call history and realize that the address she's requesting officers is actually her boyfriend's house – and he is a known drug dealer. Since drug dealers want to keep their supply safe, they often have weapons in the house – and that is information that you'd definitely want to relay to your officers before they get to the house. Most police agencies have 'briefing' before each shift and so odds are those officers are well aware of both the address and the primary occupant's history. But maybe one of those officers was on vacation on the day that the information was shared during briefing. Maybe one of the officers is a transfer from another department and so he does not yet have a history with that particular person or address.

I promise you that no officer will be upset with you for calling them before they arrive on scene to say: "I know this woman is just looking for an advisement but I'm showing her at a different address. This is her boyfriend's house and it looks like he has been known to have drugs on him or in his house in the past and he does have a weapon permit." Any officer would appreciate knowing ahead of time that there could be weapons in a house, even if the reason they're being called to that house is 'routine.' Maybe the boyfriend wasn't home when the police were called. If police are in the house talking to the woman and the boyfriend returns home and sees two police cars outside he might panic because he could think his house is being raided for drugs. He doesn't know his girlfriend called about being scammed online, so he assumes the worst and rushes in shooting. It can happen.

Always think of each and every officer's safety. One thing that helps me is thinking: "What would I want to know before getting to this complaint?" That way of thinking will help you with being a great dispatcher because you're considering the safety of the officers.

Some departments require that their new dispatchers go on ride-alongs with police officers. That's when you ride in the police car with an officer and go to calls with the officer. Ride-alongs are a great way to gain an understanding of a police officer's job. I've known some dispatchers to complain about having to run a license plate for an officer, reasoning that 'he has the same technology in his car that we have in here,' but it is a bit different running a license plate from a desk inside of a call center than it is running a license plate during a high-speed chase out there on the road! During a car chase there is so much going on: you have the chase itself so your officer is going to be calling out intersections that he's approaching or passing as well as landmarks. As his direction of travel changes, he'll be calling that out on the radio. He'll also call out his rate of speed as it changes. You'll have to acknowledge and possible repeat that information over the radio. You'll likely need to send backup officers to assist in the chase, too. Your jurisdiction is only so big though, so odds are you're going to have to call another agency to either request that they assist or to just give them a head's up that your officer is involved in a chase that is approaching their jurisdiction. So yes, running a plate in the middle of all of that might seem like a pain but you're still not running it while driving ninety-five miles per hour. If you've been on a ride-along then you'd know that there is a reason the officer is asking the dispatcher to run the plate.

Ride-alongs are also helpful for learning a jurisdiction's nooks and crannies. My jurisdiction has an alley that not many residents know about. On just one street, all of the garages are not only detached but they are also built directly behind each house. With the exception of one house, none of these houses have driveways! Just around the corner, off of a side street, there is the alley entrance. The exit of the alley? It is the one house that has a driveway on the street. It certainly is a strange set-up if you ask me, but if someone calls in the middle of the night to report a suspicious person in people's garages in this small alley then I'll know exactly where the caller means. And if an officer calls out with someone running from him in this alley I'll know that the runner has three ways out: the entrance, the exit, or through someone's yard on the street with no driveways. Every town has some hidden or little-known area like this alley. Some residents don't know that these areas even exist if they haven't been there themselves but you as a dispatcher need to know each and every one in order to effectively do your job.

Ride-alongs are a good way to not only find these places but to get a visual on their layout which can be paramount to an Officer's safety one day. Plus most agencies split up their jurisdictions or 'beats' by a few main roads and it is nice to get an in-person idea of which areas fall under which 'beat' or patrol area in case an officer needs backup because you'll know which officer is likely the closest to that area.

If your agency does not offer ride-alongs as part of the training process then ask if a ride-along system can be implemented. If your agency won't do it or can't do it then ask if you can contact a neighboring agency to do a ride-along because while you'll be seeing another jurisdiction's nooks and crannies you'll still gain an appreciation for a police officer's job – and that's what will make you great at your job as a dispatcher.

Some agencies even have citizen police academies where you learn about what the police do and why. At my agency, all dispatchers are required to go through the citizen police academy. The academy includes a tour of the police headquarters, drug awareness, car accident investigations, firearm knowledge and range time, crime scene processing, the juvenile bureau and its role, defensive tactics, criminal law, traffic law, family offenses and domestic disputes, 911 dispatch and even a K9 demonstration. A ride-along is included, too and usually a field trip to a local jail for a tour is included as well.

If a citizen police academy isn't included in your training program then find out if there is a neighboring agency that offers it because you can learn a lot of information that will be pertinent to your job as a dispatcher. A lot of times these academies are free of charge because they're meant to educate the community.

What I learned during the citizen police academy is that officers have to deal with the threat of physical violence a lot.

One officer told the class about his encounter with a man who was on drugs and had bitten this officer's ankle right through his boot. Another officer showed us how easy it was for a person to conceal a weapon. I also learned about the public's perception of the police; I was part of a demonstration where I and another participant were to sit on the ground with our arms linked as if participating in a protest that was being filmed by the news and the police wanted us to leave. In one scenario they officers grabbed our arms and legs and dragged us (across a gym mat) which would look bad to news cameras. In the other scenario, the officers activated our pressure points which allowed them to stand us up and walk us away – which looked very different than being dragged away! These academies really teach you a lot about the job of police officers which enables you to better keep their safety in mind.

Chapter Seventeen – Things Officers Really Don't Like

I mentioned to a few of my officers that I was writing an in-depth guide to dispatching, which they thought was a great idea. I told them everything that I'd be covering and I asked if they had any suggestions about what else could be included. I thought they'd suggest that I elaborate on officer safety or maybe suggest that I cover some traffic laws that dispatchers should be familiar with, but nope! They suggested that I include a chapter on things that dispatchers do that irritate officers. I jokingly told them that I could write an entire book of things that officers do that irritate dispatchers, but for police officers everywhere I am including this chapter.

The most-reported annoyance? Mic clicks. Yes, the most irritating thing that dispatchers can do is to click the mic, according to my officers. What's a mic click? It is when someone presses the 'transmit' button on the radio, but then says nothing. Or they say whatever code or phrase is used to acknowledge the officer's last transmission but they say it so quietly that the officers can't hear the dispatcher – they only hear the 'click.' I was a bit surprised that this was the most complained about, but I understand why it can irk a person. Let's say you're out on a call someplace and it is loud because people are arguing. The arguing is escalating and you call dispatch on the radio to ask for back up. The response? Click. Did the dispatcher hear you? You don't know, because all you heard was a mic click. No voice, no 'back up is en route,' nothing. So do not do 'mic clicks' and it will make officers everywhere happy! (PS – officers mic click dispatchers too – and we like it just about as much as they do).

Speaking of the radio: do not say 'um' or 'uh' in between information because that ties up radio time; keep it short and clear. Why? Because if you're droning on about something you are tying up the air which means if an officer needs to call in on the radio he can't. What if he's in trouble, and you're sending someone else to a lift assist and giving out too much information? "Patrol X, 123 Main Street for a lift assist. Uh party fell off a chair yesterday and um hurt her ankle and uh then fell again this morning but uh was able to get back up and um fell again about ten minutes ago and uh can't get up um the door is not locked uh but if it is locked see the neighbor at uh 125 Main Street um neighbor's name is Floyd." That is way too long for such a minor call, and you're giving too much information right up front. Sometimes dispatchers simply don't have very much info, especially if they receive a third party call or are dealing with a complainant who isn't very forthcoming or accommodating when asked for information – and even if dispatchers tell the officers: "No further info," the officers will ask: "Dispatch, any further info on this?" In this case, the dispatcher was smart to get the neighbor's contact information in the event a key was needed to get into the woman's house, but the dispatcher should not have tied up radio time with that information. If the officer gets to the house and it is locked then you can tell him to run next door to the neighbor's house. Know what information to put out over the radio, and when to put it out over the radio.

Another officer pet peeve: dispatchers giving every detail of the complaint and then the address of the complaint. Do not do this. Think about it: you're a police officer responding to a call. Would you rather sit stationary in your car hearing all the details and then the address you're supposed to go to, or would you rather hear the address and start driving towards it while listening to the details?

Speedy transmissions are also on the list here. If an officer is asking for information, do not give it at a rapid pace especially if that officer is going to have to write down the information. Give information at a pace that is easily heard and gives the officer time to write it down. This, like mic clicks, goes both ways. If an officer is asking for information he likely is holding a pen so he is prepared to write down that information. Some officers call into dispatch on a traffic stop, their location, and the license plate in one breath without waiting for dispatch to tell them to go ahead.

The way the transmission should go is like this:

Patrol X: "Patrol X to radio, traffic stop."

Dispatch: "Go ahead, Patrol X."

Patrol X: "Main & Center Street, Texas registration ABC 123"

Dispatch: "You're clear."

Not like this:

Patrol X: "Patrol X to radio, traffic stop Main & Center Texas registration ABC 123."

Dispatch: "Patrol X, I did not copy, repeat your location and the registration."

Contrary to popular belief, dispatchers do not sit with a pen in hand at all times. Or they may be on the phone when the officer calls in and haven't had the time to ask the person to hold so they can make sure they know where the officer is and what kind of vehicle he's out with. Yes, some patrols will be irritated to repeat themselves, but they should know better than to give all of that information when they don't know if the dispatcher is prepared to copy. Just as it takes dispatch time to write things down, it takes officers time as well – so don't rush your transmission if you're asked for information.

Another issue that officers report with dispatchers is when dispatchers send them to the wrong jurisdiction. Remember: know your jurisdiction in & out, and know your borders. Get to know your neighboring jurisdictions too so that you'll be able to direct callers to the proper agency instead of sending your officers outside of their jurisdiction.

The final complaint is not getting good descriptions. If an officer is looking for a person then he needs to know what the person is wearing, is the person is tall or short, black or white, male or female. If he's looking for a vehicle he needs to know the make & model, the color and the direction of travel.

In defense of dispatchers, though: callers are not very forthcoming about this at times. Here is an actual call I took where the caller was not very helpful despite me trying to get a good description of a person:

Dispatch: "911, what is the address of your emergency?"

Caller: "I'm at my house and this guy is outside going through garbages, he's been at it two hours now."

Dispatch: "Where is your house?"

Caller: "I don't want the police coming to my door if this guy's a nut, I don't want him knowing I called."

Dispatch: "If you do not want to see an officer that's fine but I need to know which street to send them."

Caller: "Oh right, okay I'm on Center Street two houses in from Main."

Dispatch: "What is the man wearing?"

Caller: "I don't know."

Dispatch: "Is he tall, short, young, old?"

Caller: "Look just get the cops here."

Dispatch: "They're on the way sir, but they need to know what this man looks like."

Caller: "I don't' know what he looks like!"

Dispatch: "You've been watching him for two hours, but you don't know what he looks like?"

I put the call out for Center just off Main for a suspicious male going through garbages, and once officers were on the way I said: "Be advised the caller was watching the subject for two hours but could not give a description of the male." Just so the officers know that I at least asked.

There you have it. To keep officers everywhere happy: no mic clicking and do not say 'uh' or 'um' on the radio. Give out the location of the call first and then the details of the call. Don't give out information too quickly if an officer needs to write it down. Don't send officers to jurisdictions that they don't cover. Always (try) to get a good description of a person or a vehicle.

Chapter Eighteen – Anticipating what is Needed

"You're my favorite dispatcher," "I wish all dispatchers were like you," "I hope that the new hire gets trained by you," "I love working with you," and "I wish you worked with our shift every day." These are some of the things that officers at both agencies that I work for tell me regularly and that is why in the first edition of this book this chapter was also called 'Why I am the Officers' Favorite Dispatcher.' While it is amazing to hear these things on an ongoing basis, to me I simply do my job. The first time I heard the compliments I asked what the big deal was; what set me apart from my fellow dispatchers? I was met with the same response each time: "You know what we need, sometimes before we even do!"

So what do I do that sets me apart? I know what information the officers will need and I have it ready for them before they ask for it. That's it! A big part of this job is repetition. After some time on the job, you will know what information the officers need because they will ask you for it every time.

At my agency, the officers handwrite their police reports and the dispatchers type them into the computer so that the officers can be freed up to be out on the road. Most officers do not want to sit around the station tinkering with the computers, they want to out on the road where the action is. They're better at tackling shoplifters than typing x amount of words per minute. Having typed thousands of police reports over the course of my career, I know what information is required for the reports. That is: the title of the report, complaint or report number, date and time of the incident, the location of the incident. That's followed by person information – a victim, complainant, witness, suspect, or offender's name, address, date of birth and phone number. Then vehicle information if applicable, then property information if applicable and finally the portion where the officer writes out the details of the report or the 'narrative.'

I know the information the handwritten copy of the police report is going to ask of the officer so I make sure it's printed out and even highlighted in spots to make it easier for him to do his job. Let's say the officer has arrested someone for drunk driving and the person's vehicle was towed. Because he was out on the road conducting field sobriety tests he is going to remember which tests the driver failed, not clerical things such as the time of the traffic stop.

On the clerical end though, he'll need that information for the report. The person's information, the vehicle information, which tow agency towed the car, etc. I print out the car's license plate info and the person's driver's license. These printouts have a lot of information on them but only one or two parts are needed for the police report; that's why I highlight the printouts for the officers. For the vehicle, I'll highlight '2010,' 'Ford Focus," 'blue' '4-door' and the vehicle identification number (VIN number). I won't highlight when the vehicle's registration expires or even who the registered owner is because that information isn't needed on the report and I know that. For the driver, I'll only highlight on the printout the driver's name, date of birth, and driver's license number. I'll write the complaint number on the top of the printouts as well as a physical address because when officers call out on traffic stops they give the main road and then the closest side street not an actual address – but the computer needs an actual address. By taking two seconds to look at a map, I've found the 'address of occurrence' for him, making his report that much easier to write. I even include the time of their traffic stop, the time the officer arrested the person for driving while intoxicated and the times that the person's Miranda warnings were read.

Why is printing out a few papers, highlighting them and writing a few things down so great? Because the officers need that information, they don't have to ask me for it and it's going to shorten the amount of time they take to do their report – getting them back out on the road where they want to be. Officers tell me that they have to ask other dispatchers to print out the information, then they have to ask the dispatcher what address to use, then they have to ask what the time of the traffic stop was…if someone asked me for those things once then it's a safe bet they'll always ask, right? It is better and easier for them to have the information ready – I even run it all to the booking/arrest room before they even return to the station so they don't have to come to the dispatch area to get their information.

Remember the domestic dispute call I made up earlier, the one with the man who was upset that his wife was out late and how the police were there a total of three times before someone was arrested? If my agency gets a call for a domestic dispute, I always try to get the name of both the victim and the offender. Why? Because the victim may have a stay-away restraining order/order of protection against the offender and if that is the case then someone is getting arrested. Let's say that the hypothetical wife and hypothetical husband from our earlier example were actually divorced and she had a stay-away restraining order. He would have been arrested the first time the police responded, even if she insisted that he not be arrested. Why would he be arrested? Just for being there! By being at the ex-wife's house, he is violating a judge's order – that's a big no-no and it is called Criminal Contempt. There are two kinds of these orders: stay away, which means the victim (petitioner) must not be contacted by any means by the offender (respondent) and there is a non-offensive which means the offender/respondent cannot do anything that offends the victim/petitioner. Many times even if there is not an arrest, officers complete a different kind of police report: a domestic incident report. I've seen hundreds of these reports and I know there is a portion that asks whether or not the victim now or has ever had a restraining order against the offender. That's why I get the information on the phone and look it up before the officers even get to the house – because I know they'll need that information.

I also run the driver's license of every single person an officer comes across out in the field. Why? Because if an officer pulls a vehicle over and the driver is driving with a suspended driver's license then he's going to ask me to confirm that suspension over the radio, which means that I'll need to run the license if I haven't already, then get on the air to tell him when & why the license was suspended. I'll also have to call for a tow truck so I will know ahead of time to get ready to do that.

Maybe it is not a traffic stop; maybe two officers got called to a bar to break up a fight. If the officers give me six driver's licenses to run and attach to the complaint in the computer then one of those licenses might indicate that the person is a registered sex offender who can't be within five hundred yards of a school or playground – and there's a playground across the street from the bar even if it is ten at night and the playground is empty. That person would be arrested. In some states, if a person has a restraining order against him, like our mad husband from earlier, then he cannot register or possess a firearm during the term of the restraining order. If that husband was in the bar and not involved in the fight but did call to report it: if he was found to have a firearm he'd be arrested and charged with a felony. The victim in the bar fight could have a broken nose but he could also have a warrant out for his arrest. The bartender could be a gang member! All information that would come up when I run each person's driver's license, and all information that is important to the officers on scene.

Sometimes when a business is closed for the night the wind sets off the alarm system. The alarm agency calls the police to report it and sometimes neighbors do too. Sometimes it isn't the wind; people can and do break into stores all the time. We even have the possibility of a driver losing control of her vehicle and driving right into the business. In all of those instances, we are going to need to call someone to the scene, usually who we call a 'key holder.' A key holder is an after-hours person who the police can contact in the event that the store needs attention outside of the business hours. Maybe they need to unlock the door so the police can conduct a walk-through to be sure the alarm was, in fact, a false alarm set off by the wind. Maybe the key holder is a clerk and can tell police how many packs of cigarettes were stolen, or how many scratch-off lottery tickets were stolen. Or maybe the key holder is the owner herself who needs to contact an emergency enclosure company and her business's insurance carrier because there is now a car in the middle of her store. For all of these types of calls, I'm going to find out ahead of time if there is a key holder responding, how long it will take for them to reach the scene, what their name is and what they're driving. I do this because I know that the officers responding to the call will ask me for this information so I go ahead and give it to them while they're on their way to the call.

I also look at things from a different perspective than the officers do sometimes. Just last night during an overnight shift a citizen called to report finding a lost dog. The dog was brought to the station, sometimes we'll do this in order to give the owner an opportunity to call us and locate the dog before we have to drop it off at the animal shelter. Since it was an overnight shift and I only had the minimum amount of officers working and the animal shelter is twenty miles away, we kept the dog at the station (on my lap) for about an hour. We were without a Lieutenant that night, so the most-senior officer was in charge and he decided it was time to bring the dog to the shelter. Just as he made that decision, it started pouring rain outside. We checked the surveillance cameras and saw that the street was flooding and that the community swimming pool was overflowing due to the rain. Then I took a 911 call from a resident whose basement was flooding. The most-senior officer ('acting Lieutenant') told a more junior officer to take the dog to the shelter and I interjected: "I know we're not supposed to house dogs here at the station long-term but there's only a handful of you working and we're going to get inundated with flood calls from residents and you guys may have to close the roads and direct traffic and I think it would be okay for me to watch the dog awhile so that you all can stay available." The acting Lieutenant agreed, and while they were out working in the pouring rain directing traffic and closing off roads, I had a little Shih Tzu dog sharing my chair and helping me answer all of the 911 calls for a few hours about flooded roads and basements. While the acting Lieutenant wanted to take care of the loose dog or the 'first issue,' I as a dispatcher thought ahead and knew that their resources would be better used if all of them stayed available for calls and traffic control. That's because I've worked during floods before and I know how crazy busy we can get. He agreed, and I might have saved him from a reprimand from a higher-up later on asking why it was more important for an officer to drive an already-safe dog to the animal shelter when cars were getting stuck on the flooded roads and the residents inside of them needed help.

I also give new officers a lot of help, but I do it in a respectful way that won't embarrass them. If a new officer calls out on a traffic stop with a license plate but forget to give his location, I'll say: "California registration number ABC-123, that's clear, I'm prepared to copy your location," instead of 'You need to tell me where you are, dopey!" over the radio. Sometimes a new officer will give me a police report to type and it won't have the right title or heading on it; maybe they labeled it the less-serious charge when it should have been labeled with the most serious charge. I'll call their cell phone and ask if they mind if I change it for them, and normally they'll run back to the station and change it themselves or rewrite the report and they always thank me profusely because the 'rough draft' didn't make it to the Lieutenant for review. I want them to succeed and if I can help then I will.

Anticipating what the officers will need, especially if it makes them more informed and feel safer: that is the difference between a dispatcher and a great dispatcher.

Part 7 –

Dispatcher Conduct, Dispatcher Safety

and Social Media

Chapter Nineteen – Ethics & Confidentiality

Once an elderly man showed up at my agency with a suitcase and asked me through the window to call him a taxi to take him to the airport. This isn't something that a dispatcher would be expected or required to do but I wasn't busy so I did so for him. A while later our maintenance man was cleaning the front hallway and said: "Hey, that old man left you $10 as a tip!" and handed it to me. Because I'm not an officer I'm not held to the same set of rules and regulations as the officers are but as a representative of the station I did not feel right accepting that ten dollar bill. Plus I did not notice the elderly man leaving it there; it was possible that he intended to use it towards his cab fare or it could have been dropped at any point during the day by anyone in that hallway. I put it in an envelope with a note explaining the chain of events and left the envelope for my Lieutenant. He forwarded the money and note to the Captain who then returned to me the $10 with a note saying that I was right to not accept/keep the money and because I had turned it in and did the right thing I was entitled to keep the money. I donated the money anyway, but I figured that it was not right for me to keep it initially so I did the right thing and turned it into someone higher-up than me. That's ethical and I would hope that all dispatchers would do the same if the public ever tries to tip them. Ethics are important, especially in law enforcement jobs.

True story: once, while at mandatory training I was told the tale of a dispatcher who was a huge fan of an unnamed celebrity. Having just purchased some merchandise of this celebrity's, the dispatcher really wanted to have it signed by the celebrity. So this dispatcher used police software to run the celebrity for a driver's license in order to find out the celebrity's address. The plan was to show up at the celebrity's home and ask for an autograph. I heard this tale quite a long time ago so I can't remember where this happened or what the outcome was. If I had to guess, I'd imagine that particular dispatcher will never work as a civil servant again. The point of this tale being told at training was to warn us: certain people's names are 'flagged' in the system. If you run the name of a celebrity of any sort, odds are they are flagged. Immediately after performing the search, your department's supervisory staff will receive a report of who requested that person's information and then you'll likely lose your job. Famous or not, everyone is entitled to their privacy. Using your dispatcher role and your department's computer software to gain personal information about a celebrity or public figure is extremely unethical – especially if it for any reason other than a professional reason. If your patrol conducts a traffic stop and asks you to run a driver's license and the driver ends up being the President of the United States: that's okay to do because you were asked to do so. But if you just run the President's name for 'fun' or some other non-work reason then you're going to be found out – so don't do it!

There are other people that you should not attempt to gain information about, too; it is not just celebrities and public figures that you should not look up.

Look at the scenarios below and decide in which situations it is okay to do some checking out of a person:

1) Your uncle owns a rental property and a prospective tenant seemed nice to him but he feels that the person is 'off' somehow or is hiding something. He asks you to check at work to find out if the prospective tenant has any warrants.

2) Your 18-year old daughter is dating a much older man and you think he seems violent and you want to see if he's ever been arrested for any violent crimes. The next time you're at work, you pop his name in the system to ensure that he's not a criminal because you want to protect your daughter.

3) A friend that lives near your ex-husband confides in you that the police were at your ex-husband's house over the weekend. You are curious about what, so once you're at work you put in his address to find out what happened and share your findings with your friend.

4) An off-duty detective calls you from the mall on his day off and gives you a license plate number to run because there is a dog in a car with no open windows and it is ninety degrees outside.

5) An officer from an out-of-state agency calls and asks that you provide a phone number for the family member of a victim of a fatal motor vehicle accident.

So, how did you do? If you determined that scenarios #1, #2, and #3 are absolute no-no's: then you are 100% correct. None of these scenarios have anything to do with your job and they're all one form or another of personal gain.

If the uncle in scenario #1 wanted to find out about a prospective tenant's possible warrants or criminal history then he can pay an agency to conduct a background check. In scenario #2 you may be very tempted to find out if the daughter's boyfriend has a criminal history but it isn't right or ethical to do so. Finding out personal information about the ex-husband in scenario #3 is not ethical, either and neither would be sharing your findings with your friend. In fact, that would be a huge breach of confidentiality.

Scenarios #4 and #5 are trickier. If you are a seasoned dispatcher then you likely know your patrols' and detectives' voices just as well as your own so it is very easy for you to verify that you are speaking with an actual detective that is known to you. And since the dog in scenario #4 is in danger you should absolutely be able to run the plate for the detective in order for him to locate the owner by name inside of the mall. However, if you're a new dispatcher then you're probably not familiar with a lot of the detectives' voices and should probably have that person talk to a higher-up for verification so that it isn't you on the line if the person is not, in fact, law enforcement. Scenario #5 happens more frequently than you'd imagine; victims of fatalities often have family members or next of kin in other states who need to be notified in the event of their deaths. And more than likely, your department would attempt to notify the family in person and not over the phone.

What information would you want to be provided about you to a person? Maybe an ex-colleague didn't care for you and you got arrested for shoplifting...if that person called the police department asking about your arrest, would you want that person knowing about your charges? Of course not, and neither do the people who are arrested by your department. At my agency, we never give out arrest information over the phone. One reason is that we can't verify who we are speaking with. If someone is under arrest in the evening and is being held until a judge can arraign him in the morning, then that person may miss work in the morning. Let's say someone calls claiming to be that person's boss and he's asking about the arrestee – do you give this caller any information about the arrestee? I sure wouldn't, because I don't know that it is, in fact, the person's boss. For all I know it could be the new boyfriend of the arrestee's ex-girlfriend on the phone. If an officer wants to provide that information to a caller, that's fine. But as a dispatcher, I don't do it without a higher-up's green light to do so.

Confidentiality doesn't just pertain to arrestees. Think of all the calls you take in a shift: a lot of the times, complainants do not want to be identified. Usually, it is a neighbor calling in a noise complaint and they all say the same thing: "I don't want my neighbor knowing it was me who called…" is how a lot of calls start out. Those callers are entitled to confidentiality. Maybe someone you went to college with got arrested for drunk driving while you were working. That isn't something you'd share at a reunion because it would be a breach of confidentiality. Most dispatchers also have access to police reports and arrest records and at some point, you will come across the name of someone you know; maybe it is a friend of yours, even. It would still never be appropriate to discuss that confidential information with that friend or with anyone outside of the department. Maybe a handful of your neighbors know that you work for a police department, and one day an ambulance or fire truck is at a house down the block from you. The next day those neighbors might ask you what happened at that house, and you should not fill them in because that would be a breach of confidentiality especially if you were not even working during the event and if you looked up the information the next time you were at work specifically to obtain it in order to inform your neighbors.

It is likely that your department has a policy in place about what information you may release to whom. If I am out with friends and they ask me if I've had any 'crazy phone calls' lately I will occasionally share some of the ridiculous calls but I strategically leave out certain information. Just today I took a 911 call from a woman who was walking her dog and while crossing a driveway, the homeowner was pulling into that driveway and he told her to 'do that at the dog park.' The woman thought that this was 'threatening.' It gets better: the incident occurred yesterday and she was calling 911 a full day later to report it. 911 is for emergencies, not for day-old complaints about mean comments. And, I secretly suspect that her dog had defecated on the lawn and that is what prompted the man to say anything to her at all. I'm not sure what she expected the police to do about her 'predicament,' because no laws were broken. The police don't throw people in jail for not wanting dog feces on their lawn or saying mean things. Notice that during this story I did not say the name of the woman or the homeowner; I only used 'she' and 'he.' I did not even say the name of the street this occurred on. That way my friends still get a laugh out of it but I haven't revealed any confidential information about any of the parties involved. Sometimes I'll tell friends that I've only had routine calls because you never know when someone will know the person that I'm talking about and even if it is something comical that doesn't mean the person will appreciate any details being openly discussed with anyone.

Chapter Twenty – Dispatcher Safety

Dispatcher safety? Why would there be a chapter about dispatcher safety? Aren't dispatchers safe inside of the centers that they work in? Yes, but also no.

Some dispatchers are responsible for watching and checking on prisoners. Usually, a prisoner is inside of his own locked cell. The cell itself is one of ten or twelve cells which are all behind a locked gate or door. Some have this gated area inside of another larger area with an additional locked door, so the prisoners are triple-locked in. Most holding cells have surveillance cameras in them but many states require that prisoners be checked in person about every half hour or so. If you work at a police station that also houses prisoners then it may be your responsibility to check on those prisoners. At my agency there is a line painted on the floor in the cell block; it runs parallel with the cells. I never step over that line because it designates the average male's arm reach. Many people who are arrested are not happy about it and would do anything to get out of that cell, so what's to stop a motivated prisoner from reaching through the bars to grab my head and slam it into the bars in order to knock me out and steal the keys? Never ever get that close to a prisoner, even if they're behind bars because you don't know what they'll do if they're able to get their hands on you.

We also have a booking/arrest processing room and occasionally I will be asked to bring the officer in that room some paperwork that he needs in order to do his job. There is a prisoner bench fitted with handcuffs and that's typically where prisoners are: handcuffed to that bench. However, most prisoners are still able to stand up, reach and kick and for that reason I never walk even close to that bench. Other times the officer will have the prisoner not handcuffed during the fingerprinting or mug shot process and in those cases, I'll wait to go in the room at all. A lot of the police officers at my agency are really good about dispatcher safety; if an officer is bringing a prisoner into the police station and I happen to be in a hallway and it's unavoidable that I'll pass that officer and prisoner then the officer will always put himself between me and the prisoner for my safety.

Besides within the walls of your agency or call center, where else do you need to worry about being safe? Depending on your department-issued uniform and what it looks like, you very may well 'look' like a police officer. If you're stopping at the gas station before work and gassing up your car in full uniform then the public is going to think that you are a police officer. What if someone at the gas station has been arrested in the past and that person now has a personal vendetta against police officers? Are you safe? What if someone inside of the gas station commits a robbery and other customers run to you for help, assuming that you're a police officer and that you can stop that person? It is for these reasons that I never wear my full uniform while in public. I would not want to be mistaken for a police officer in any situation.

I look at it this way: if I'm in uniform then I am a representative of my police agency. Even if I'm not giving a press release or interview for a news company (something a dispatcher would never do) I am still representing my agency. So stopping at a liquor store after work to pick up a bottle of wine on my way to a friend's birthday party while in uniform isn't something that I'd want to do because to some people that might look like I'm drinking on the job. I'd also never meet up with friends for happy hour in my uniform. Even if I'm stopping at a restaurant or pizza place before work to grab something quick to eat: I never wear my uniform because I don't want to be mistaken for a police officer. At a restaurant especially I won't wear my uniform because two possible scenarios could happen: 1) the staff may not be fans of law enforcement and that same staff is handing my food or 2) the staff may appreciate law enforcement and may offer to feed me for free. In most agencies, it is forbidden to accept gifts, tips or services of any kind from the public and that includes free food.

The instant people see you in a uniform they will want to approach you with questions about parking tickets, civil issues, etc. Do you really want to be bothered with all of that during your time off from work? I know I don't!

There are many reasons to not wear your uniform in public or while out running errands, but aside from off-site training or workshops/conferences I can't think of a single good reason to wear your uniform outside of your station or call center.

Chapter Twenty-Two – Social Media

I have social media accounts, but I do not list my employer or my line of work on social media. I am friends with colleagues (both dispatchers and officers) on social media and a lot of them use pseudonyms instead of their real names, and they also don't list their place of employment or line of work. Why? Because in today's day and age where a lot of people have a disrespect or even a hate for law enforcement, attorneys representing their clients will summon your social media accounts just as quickly as they might summon a patrol car's surveillance camera, an officer's body camera footage, or a recording of a 911 call.

There are people out there who will (and do) create fake profiles by stealing an officer's name and photos. Yes, my family and friends know what I do and where I work but I don't list that information online because I don't want to ever have my private life under scrutiny by anyone out there in the world.

I never share work-related information on social media. There have been law enforcement workers who have been terminated for sharing work-related information on social media and that includes both officers and dispatchers. That could be a dispatcher posting information about a 911 call or an officer posting something that someone considers to be offensive. Just like wearing your uniform outside of work makes you appear as a representative for your agency, social media posts by a civil servant can appear (like it or not) to be connected to your agency.

There are exceptions. If an officer finds a lost dog I may snap a picture of it and post the photo in a community page for lost and found pets on Facebook – but that's me doing that as a citizen, not as a dispatcher for my agency. If anyone online that I am not 'friends' with were to click on my name there would be no indication that I am a civil servant or where I work. And because my privacy settings are high, no one can see any of my posts, friends, or photos on my profile anyhow. I may receive an Amber Alert at work for a missing or abducted child and I certainly will not post that information online whereas if I come across a post online I will 'share' it. My agency has a social media page, and if they post a job then I will 'share' it. If I come across a positive news story about my agency or any neighboring agencies I will 'share' those as well.

There is a website relating to lost/found/stolen cameras. If you've lost your camera you can upload a saved photo that you've taken on that camera to this website and it will scan the internet and alert you if any new photos taken with that camera were posted anywhere online. It uses the camera's unique 'serial number' so to speak in order to coordinate all of this. Photos can also be geotagged, meaning people are able to determine where a photo was taken. That means that the holiday photo that you took on your cell phone of your family outside of your residence with the holiday lights could potentially reveal the exact location of your house to anyone who knows how to look. That isn't information that any officer or dispatcher wants the public having access to.

There's also facial recognition software out there. If you have a Facebook account and you post a photo of you and some friends, Facebook can automatically suggest that you 'tag' your friends using their facial recognition software. There is similar technology out there and it isn't uncommon for criminals to take photos of police officers in the line of duty or even new police academy graduates right at the ceremony to collect intelligence on officers. Additionally, a person can save an officer's profile picture on social media.

Intelligence gathering goes both ways, though. I've received BOLOs or ATLs ('be on the lookout' and 'attempt to locate') from other agencies while at work and I'll certainly use Facebook to try and find a photo of the person to make it easier for my officers to identify that person should they come across him or her. Once I found a photo of a person who was a suspect in a case and the photo I printed out exactly matched a surveillance photo, the person was even wearing the same clothing in both photos.

One more note on social media – be mindful of what you post and share. Besides not ever sharing work-related information, you should also not post anything inappropriate or potentially offensive. Ask yourself before you post something: who might not approve of this? Would your spouse approve? How about your parents? What about your chief of police – would he approve? If you aren't sure if you should post something on social media then you probably should not be posting it.

Part 8 - Resources

Chapter Twenty-Two – Drugs

I believe I mentioned that one of my officers once had a man high on drugs and the man bit my officer on the ankle right through the officer's duty boot, and those boots are thick! Certain drugs make people do crazy things. Any number of drugs could have caused this man to have had such super strength. In this chapter, we'll cover some commonly-used drugs and their effects on people.

Flakka. Google 'zombie drug' and look for some videos of people on the drug called 'Flakka,' it is crazy how unpredictable this drug makes people. It is also called 'the insanity drug.' People who are on it really do look like zombies the way they walk and maneuver – they're slow and seem out of it, often walking while bending over forwards at the waist with their heads toward the ground. But other times they're in a full run. They have hallucinations and they become paranoid. They jump through windows without appearing to sustain any injuries and they can become incredibly violent. Flakka raises a person's body temperature so much that many users take off their clothes while high on Flakka. When someone on this drug becomes combative, it sometimes takes six or more officers to subdue these people. Flakka is a synthetic drug that is more powerful than cocaine or heroin and it is relatively cheap ($5) to buy. People take it by mixing it with a liquid such as water and drinking it, or snorting it, or smoking it, or injecting it, or taking it in tablet form. Needless to say, it makes people potentially very dangerous to the community and to responding emergency personnel.

Cocaine. This drug causes the user to be to be very energetic and talkative, and people on it appear to be very 'pumped up,' often with dilated pupils. People who use cocaine regularly have behavioral signs of such including paranoia, excessive aggression, hallucinations, delusional thoughts and a lack of judgment. Sometimes users get a runny nose and/or nosebleeds, as this drug is snorted up the nose.

Crack. This is a form of cocaine that can be smoked, it is also referred to as 'crack cocaine.' Crack is said to produce a sense of euphoria, which explains why it is so addictive. A crack high is a very intense high but it is short-lived. Tell-tale signs of a person being a crack user are burns on their fingers or lips (from smoking the crack out of a pipe), amplified aggression, hallucinations, and mood swings.

Depressants. Depressants are legal if they are prescribed to a person, but many people steal these drugs and use them illegally. Commonly-abused depressants are generally prescribed to treat anxiety and panic disorders and include brand names such as Xanax, Valium, and Klonopin. Depressants cause feelings of elation but also extreme drowsiness.

Fentanyl. Fentanyl is an opioid that is often made illegally and is mixed with cocaine or heroin. Medially, it is a narcotic pain reliever that is used following a surgery to help alleviate pain. It is about 50-100 times stronger than morphine. When used incorrectly or illegally, a very small amount of fentanyl can be fatal. Illegally manufactured fentanyl comes in patch form, tablet form, spray form and lozenge form. People who use this drug often report it makes them feel a rush of euphoria. Tell-tale signs of someone on fentanyl is weakness and trouble walking, slurred speech, drowsiness, pinpoint-sized pupils, hallucinations and a slower rate of breathing.

Ketamine. Ketamine is usually a drug used for animals, but people use it to achieve a dream-like state however it can also cause hallucinations. It can be injected, consumed in drinks, snorted or added to cigarettes or to marijuana joints. Ketamine has been used as the 'date rape' drug because users of the drug find it difficult to move.

LSD. LSD (lysergic acid diethylamide) is a hallucinogenic drug. This drug was more popular in the 1960's to the 1980's but it remains to be used today. People on LSD may see or hear things that do not exist and other effects include altered thoughts and feelings. Typically, someone on LSD will have dilated pupils, increased blood pressure and an increased body temperature.

MDMA. MDMA (methylenedioxy-methamphetamine) is a synthetic drug also known as 'ecstasy' or 'molly.' It produces feelings of increased energy and was very popular in the 1990's dance clubs and 'raves.' It produces feelings of pleasure and emotional warmth as well as a distorted sense of time perception. It comes in tablet form, liquid form, and powder form so it can be ingested or snorted. MDMA can cause chills, sweating, blurred vision, teeth clenching, nausea and muscle cramping.

Mescaline. Another hallucinogen, this drug comes from a peyote cactus but it can also be produced synthetically. The drug is generally soaked in water or chewed and produces an effect which lasts for up to twelve hours. Users of this drug typically experience hallucinations and dream-like feelings but can also experience dizziness, diarrhea, vomiting, anxiety and a racing heart rate.

Methamphetamine. Also known as 'crystal meth,' 'crank,' 'speed' and 'ice,' methamphetamine is a stimulant drug that usually comes in powder or pill form but it can also be smoked, snorted or injected. People who use meth experience extreme weight loss, dental problems ("meth mouth") and intense itching that can lead to skin sores due to excessive scratching. You can Google: 'meth: before and after' and look at mug shots/arrest photos of methamphetamine users; their faces are often covered in skin sores and their mouths are sunken in due to deteriorating teeth. Users can also experience hallucinations, sleeping problems, paranoia and violent behavior.

Opium. Opium is made from the poppy plant and it is an opioid or narcotic. It looks like a brown or black block of tar-like powder, and it comes in liquid form as well. Opium can be smoked, taken in pill form or injected. It can cause a feeling of euphoria and a sedated effect that feels like a calm drowsiness. Large doses can cause a person's breathing to slow down and even stop and combining opium with alcohol can make this a bigger likelihood.

PCP. PCP or 'phencyclidine' is another illegal hallucinogenic street drug. It comes in powder or liquid and it can be snorted, injected, smoked or swallowed. Other names for PCP are 'angel dust' and 'rocket fuel.' People who use PCP feel as if they're floating and they feel a sense of euphoria. They also experience less inhibition, similar to being intoxicated. People on PCP also can feel fearless and that they have superhuman strength.

Psilocin and Psilocybin. Psilocin and psilocybin are hallucinogenic compounds that are contained in certain mushrooms. Also known as 'mushrooms' or 'shrooms,' these can produce a feeling of euphoria. Signs that someone is on mushrooms is dilated pupils, impaired motor skills, rapid breathing, and hostility.

Ritalin. Ritalin is another legal drug when prescribed (to treat Attention Deficit Hyperactivity Disorder or ADHD), but it is often abused by people who want to get high, lose weight or improve their alertness/stay awake. Popular among students it is referred to as a 'smart drug' due to having a reputation to improve academic performance. It can be swallowed, snorted, or injected and produces a feeling of euphoria. People on Ritalin may have dilated pupils, weight loss, headaches, sweating, insomnia, rapid heart rate and impaired vision.

Adderall. Adderall is [prescribed to treat ADHD and sometimes to treat sleep disorders. Adderall can be snorted or taken in tablet or capsule form. Like Ritalin, people take this drug to stay awake and study longer to improve their academic performance, but it is also can be used by those with eating disorders because it can suppress the appetite. Signs of use include a headache, dry mouth, hoarse voice, nausea and diarrhea or constipation. Some users will stay awake for days at a time and then 'crash' where they are very lethargic and in a depressed-like state.

Rohypnol. About 10 times more potent than Valium, Rohypnol is a tranquilizer. It comes in pill form and users either crush and snort it, sprinkle it and smoke it with marijuana, or dissolve it to inject or mix with a drink. Commonly known as a 'roofie' this is another 'date rape' drug because it renders the victim incapable of resisting a sexual assault. People who use Rohypnol experience a loss of muscle control, confusion, drowsiness, and amnesia. These effects take place about twenty minutes after taking the drug and the effects can last as long as twelve hours. Afterward, the drug wears off, the person may not be able to recall anything that occurred during that time period.

If someone calls 911 and reports someone acting violently, irrationally or otherwise it is always a good idea to ask if the caller knows if the person has taken any drugs (or drank any alcohol) and if the caller knows what kind of drugs were taken by the person. Drugs can be an officer safety issue due to the effects such as a person having superhuman strength. A drug such as a Fentanyl can cause an officer to overdose if he comes in contact with it, making drugs an even bigger officer safety issue.

Chapter Twenty-Three - Vehicle Abbreviations

Every license plate has a 'plate type' which designates what sort of vehicle it is or suggests what the vehicle is used for. While not a complete list, here are some commonly used abbreviations:

AT   All-terrain vehicle

AM   Ambulance

AQ   Antique, classic, collectible

BU   Bus

CI   City-owned or municipal vehicle

CO   Commercial

DL   Dealer

DP   Diplomatic

DX   Disabled person

EX   Exempt

FM   Farm vehicle

FD   Fire department

JJ   Judge or justice

LF   Law enforcement

MP   Moped
MC   Motorcycle

PH   Doctor
PP   Passenger

RV   Rented vehicle or trailer

SN   Snowmobile

TL   Trailer
TK   Truck
TR   Semi truck
TX   Cab

Additionally, all vehicles are assigned a 'style' and here is a list of the abbreviations of those styles:

2D   Sedan (2-door)

3D   3-door

4D   4-door

BZ   Biohazard

BT   Boat trailer

CT   Camping

DS   Tractor truck

LL   Carry-all

CV   Convertible

DP   Dump truck

FB   Flatbed

HR   Hearse

HP   Helicopter

LM   Limousine

MH   Motorized home

PK   Pickup

SQ   Search and rescue

SD   Sedan (2 doors)

UV   Utility vehicle

UT   Utility trailer

Chapter Twenty-Four – State and Province Abbreviations

A lot of the license plates that you'll be asked to run will be from your own state, but there are times that you'll need to run an out-of-state license plate and for that, you'll need the state's abbreviation.

Here is a list of those abbreviations:

AL   Alabama

AK   Alaska

AZ   Arizona

AR   Arkansas

CA   California

CO   Colorado

CT   Connecticut

DE   Delaware

DC   District of Columbia

FL   Florida

GA   George

HI   Hawaii

ID Idaho

IL Illinois

IN Indiana

IA Iowa

KS Kansas

KY Kentucky

LA Louisiana

ME Maine

MD Maryland

MA Massachusetts

MI Michigan

MN Minnesota

MO Missouri

MT Montana

NB Nebraska

NC North Carolina

ND North Dakota

NV Nevada

NH New Hampshire

NJ New Jersey

NY New York

OH Ohio

OK Oklahoma

OR Oregon

PA Pennsylvania

RI Rhode Island

SC South Carolina

SD South Dakota

TN Tennessee

TX Texas

UT Utah

VT Vermont

VA Virginia

WA Washington

WV   West Virginia

WI   Wisconsin

WY   Wyoming

Additionally, most agencies are able to run license plates in certain USA commonwealths, such as Puerto Rico (PR).

For Canadian plates you must enter the Province, here is a list of those Provinces:

AB   Alberta

BC   British Columbia

MB   Manitoba

NK   New Brunswick

NF   Newfoundland

NS   Nova Scotia

NT   Northwest Territories

ON   Ontario

PE   Prince Edward Island

PQ   Quebec

SK   Saskatchewan

YK   Yukon Territory

Chapter Twenty-Five - Learn How to Do Your Job

Nearly every agency has a training program that new dispatchers must complete before they can be sent out on their own to take emergency calls. This can be an off-site program or the training can take place in real time at the call center or agency you'll be working for, or a combination of the two options.

Generally, outside of any off-site training, a new dispatcher will train at the call center or the police station that they'll be working in. He will observe a senior dispatcher/training dispatcher performing his job to get an idea of what goes on during a typical shift. Then he will listen in on non-emergency calls as well as 911 calls to see how different types of calls are handled. The trainee needs to familiarize himself with the computer software that the agency uses; some agencies have software that allows new dispatchers to create 'test' complaints in the computer and there are 'dummy' license plates that can be run in the system, too. The new dispatcher will basically learn things in 'blocks': phones, computers, radio, etc. Then they will go from only answering phones to both answering the phones and generating complaints in the computer. After a while, they will be doing everything at once, which is what dispatching is really like.

New dispatchers are usually intimidated to answer 911 calls at first, understandably. Some call centers are quieter than others 911-wise so a new hire may not get the opportunity to answer many 911 calls during the training process before they're 'on their own' and responsible for those 911 lines. I've had dispatchers ask me how they can get experience with 911 calls if not many 911 calls are taken during the training process.

Some agencies work off of a computer program that prompts the dispatcher which questions to ask or what to tell the caller, some agencies work off similar 'flip cards' and some agencies use nothing but common sense. If your agency uses the computer program or flip cards, I'd recommend reviewing those until you have a very good idea of their layout and how the questions flow.

If your agency doesn't use anything official then I'd recommend going on YouTube. Seriously! If you search '911' on YouTube, you can listen to 911 calls that range from very funny to very serious. That will give you a great idea of how to (and how not to) handle various 911 calls. One particular YouTube channel, PSTC, (Public Safety Training Consultants) has 'two-minute training' videos which cover a variety of topics.

During your training, don't be afraid to ask questions even if you think that they're basic questions. When I started, I didn't know what the chain of command looked like so I asked my trainer if a Lieutenant was 'higher' on the chain than a Captain is (nope). I asked what happens if we get a 911 hang-up (we send a patrol car to the caller's location to conduct a welfare check). I asked which is more important: the radio traffic or 911 calls (that depends on the severity of the 911 call as well as the seriousness of the radio traffic). Asking questions is a good thing; I always shudder a bit inside when I ask trainees who have no experience with dispatching if they have any questions and they just shake their heads 'no.' How can someone not have any questions at all?

Another thing that I don't see trainees doing at times is taking notes, even after I've prompted them to do so. This is a serious job, there isn't much room for winging it. Once you're on your own there will not be someone right there with you to answer questions, so where will you turn if you need answers? You'll refer back to your notes!

Here are some examples of things that you may want to find out during your training period:

How do you find an Order of Protection?

How can you find out if a person has a warrant?

What is the police department's role in the event that a vehicle is repossessed from the registered owner by a repossession agency?

Where do you find the contact information for employees of a business that you may have to contact after-hours?

If your job involves typing police reports: who in the station gets a copy of the completed reports?

Can complaints in the computer be deleted or merged if a clerical mistake is made or if there are duplicate complaints about the same call?

If you're responsible for making the 'line-up' of patrols in the computer at the start of new shift: how do you do that?

Does your agency use a towing service and if so: are the towed vehicles recorded or entered somewhere?

How can you run a license plate by the VIN number instead of the license plate?

If you're responsible for entering missing persons into the computer system: how do you do that? How about stolen vehicles, notifications of robberies or stolen firearms or other property?

How do you transfer a caller to someone else's desk or voicemail box?

How do you transfer a 911 call to another agency?

What's the radio code for asking an officer his location?

Under what circumstances would you send a police officer to another jurisdiction's complaint?

What do you do if your computers go down?

How do you use the TTY feature on 911 calls for hearing-impaired callers?

Does your agency deal with animals running at large?   How about with wildlife? What about injured animals?

Who do you notify if a traffic signal is out/ not functioning properly?

If you're responsible for checking prisoners and one tries to hang himself in the cell: what do you do?

How do you find out the backup address of a residence or of a business in the event that someone running from police officers hops a fence?

Does your agency help people who are locked out of their vehicles or out of their homes?

If your agency uses surveillance cameras: how do you adjust them? Do you have the ability to go back a few minutes to look for the license plate on a vehicle that left the scene of a bank robbery?

Those are the types of questions that new dispatchers should be asking, among others that may come up that are more specific to whichever agency the dispatcher trainee is working for.

Epilogue

I hope that this book has helped in preparing you to be the best dispatcher that you can be. So much goes into this job and a lot of the information that gets thrown at new hires can be overwhelming at times. In a way that's a good thing because it prepares us to deal with those shifts that are insanely busy and we're multi-tasking like crazy and making split-second decisions every minute.

Nothing can truly prepare a person to be a dispatcher. When I started I thought that all 911 calls were life-or-death emergencies; I had no idea that nine out of every ten 911 calls I'd take would be from people whose feelings were hurt by a restaurant manager or by a neighbor, or calls from people with other issues that were far from emergencies. I never imagined working during a flood in my area but it has happened. Dispatchers have to go to work just like doctors and firefighters and other emergency personnel; work will find a way to get us there because we're going to be needed in events such as natural disasters.

There are some pretty nice perks about being a dispatcher. You know about big crimes before the media does, which is kind of neat. You also have job security because people will always need to contact the police for one reason or another. If you're lucky you work for an agency that gives you benefits and allows you to participate in the police retirement plan. And let's not forget the number of people that you get to help during each and every shift! Dispatching really can be a very fulfilling and rewarding career.

Made in the USA
Las Vegas, NV
19 August 2022

53615951R00080